Hymns as Poetry

Hymns as Poetry

An Anthology compiled by

TOM INGRAM

and

DOUGLAS NEWTON

CONSTABLE · LONDON

LONDON
PUBLISHED BY
Constable and Company Ltd
10–12 ORANGE STREET W.C.2
·

INDIA
Orient Longmans Ltd
BOMBAY   CALCUTTA   MADRAS
·

CANADA
Longmans, Green and Company
TORONTO
·

SOUTH AND EAST AFRICA
Longmans, Green and Company Ltd
CAPETOWN   NAIROBI
·

AUSTRALIA
Walter Standish and Sons
SYDNEY

First published 1956

Made and printed in Great Britain by
William Clowes and Sons, Limited, London and Beccles

TO

BARBARA JONES AND MARY LEE SETTLE

Acknowledgments

IT is a pleasant duty to offer our thanks to those who have helped to make this book possible. We are grateful to Mr John Betjeman for his generous and helpful advice in the early stages of the planning of it.   Like innumerable others, we are particularly indebted to the librarians and staff of the British Museum Reading Room; without the facilities and extraordinary resources of that institution, and the patience and helpfulness of those who work there, our project would have been far harder and less pleasant to carry out.

We must thank Messrs. Marshall, Morgan & Scott Ltd. for permission to reprint Frances J. Crosby's hymns, *Come, oh come with thy broken heart* and *Saved by Grace*; and G. Bennard's *The Old Rugged Cross* is used by permission of its owner, the Rodeheaver Company (Copyright 1941, Renewal).

All efforts have been made to trace owners of rights in the hymns which we have chosen. In the event that any have been overlooked, or suitable acknowledgments omitted, we ask that our apologies should be accepted.

Preface

THE definition of a hymn which we have used to guide us in selection is discussed in the Introduction. Here it suffices to say to those people who find the Moravian, or some of the nineteenth-century Revival pieces, worrying, that our title "Hymns as Poetry" has been the real guide. Poetry can cover every shade of emotion and thought, and every part of the universe, and the hymn, which uses the same part of the mind as the poem for its composition, covers every aspect of God's praise, and it is impossible to confine this anthology to hymns to the Trinity or the Holy Ghost, or for Christmas or for Shipwrecked Sailors or by Roman Catholics or by Nonconformists.

The dates and the division of the poems into sections must also be explained. The reason for starting with Kethe and the Wedderburns is an historical one. In the middle of the sixteenth century English had emerged as the language we know today. Before that date it was a language in a state of rapid evolution, and literary history regards the period up to the middle of the sixteenth century as one in which the language was established. We have chosen to start at a time when the language was established; an anthology of English hymns written before 1540 would be a different work, clotted with glossaries to make the poems intelligible to the general reader.

The sixteenth, seventeenth and eighteenth centuries have been divided denominationally to show the main streams of hymn writing which joined in the nineteenth century. The nineteenth-century hymns, with the exception of the revivalist ones, are put together. By then hymn singing had become established as a part of worship in almost every church in

England. The number of hymns written was immense, and for the first time in her history the Church of England supported the singing of new hymns, with the result that clerical poets were sanctioned to express their religious feelings in song, and even if few have survived criticism and time, they were a noble army of writers although many are only remembered for one work. This was also the great century for compilations. There were hymn books for sailors, hospitals, Sunday schools, feast days; almost every aspect of religious life was commemorated by a special hymnal, produced either for the use of special congregations, or by clergymen of the established church and by other priests and ministers. These books are the despair of the anthologist. Many of them (to be convenient for the reticule) are tiny, only a few inches either way, tight little books which are always trying to close themselves like mouse-traps. Their bindings, however, are almost always beautiful, rich, red, green and violet papers; some of the smarter books, out of the penny Sunday school hymnal class, are illustrated with chalky lithographs of a dove, little girls in muffs, or a prickly spray of blackberries. But all of these contain the same hymns. Each denomination used the best hymns of the others, rewriting objectionable passages. The result is that if the confusion were to be sorted out, the part of the anthology containing the nineteenth-century hymns would be a chaos of subheadings and divisions. So the hymns have been arranged chronologically irrespective of denomination.

One more point remains; the reason for stopping at the end of the nineteenth century. The nineteenth century was one of the most fertile periods for poetry in our literary history, a period of experiment and invention, with literature more closely integrated with religion than it is now. The period starts vigorously, proceeds to a great climax and then dies down in a succession of isolated masterpieces. To continue the selection into the twentieth century would make the anthology end with a whimper. The development of the gospel song is also another reason for ending when we do. The initiative passed from the established churches and established denominations of non-conformity in about 1870 to the revivalists, and just as an anthology on our premises makes hymns before 1540 a separate book, so must the gospel song be separated; it, like the carol, is not a hymn. Omissions within the framework which we established for ourselves are due to taste. Often if old favourites are not here it is because their splendour lies in their tunes. Think of them without their tunes; think of them as poems.

Contents

Introduction

WHAT is a hymn? Generally speaking we associate the word with a religious song of praise performed by the congregation as part of a service; and generally speaking we are right to do so. But a closer examination of actual hymns brings to light a number of interesting facts. Many hymns are not devoted entirely to praise of God: they are expressions of repentance or foreboding, or appeals for deliverance from evils or the prospect of evils. They cover, in fact, a multitude of occasions and contingencies, not all of which are specifically religious in tone. Many trespass on the provinces of the psalm or even of the scriptural text which they paraphrase closely. Many are addressed to the Lord not as from the congregation collectively, but from individuals. Besides this, there are poems entitled "hymns" by their authors—Milton's *Hymn on the Morning of Christ's Nativity* is a familiar example —which not only are clearly unsuitable for singing, but were never for a moment intended to be sung. There are, too, numerous hymns in use which prove, on investigation, to be poems whose authors never intended them to be anything else, but which have been lifted from their original contexts by compilers of hymn-books and adapted to their purpose with such success that their origins are practically forgotten.

All these considerations had to be borne in mind during the making of this anthology. Ultimately the acid tests have been the questions: "Does this express any kind of relationship between the worshipper and God?" and "Was this hymn ever sung, or was it at least written for singing?" The answers to the second question have led to some surprises and have led to some interesting discoveries: as that John Donne's "Wilt Thou forgive", so strong in Donne's typically personal and passionate

I

feeling, was in fact sung before him at St. Paul's. At the same time, it is in making this particular test that we have allowed ourselves a certain latitude. We have had no qualms over including numbers of hymns which certainly have never been sung, because they were the work of writers whose thoughts were concentrated on the writing of hymns, and quantities of whose poems were immediately put to use: so that, in effect, almost any poem they had written which has not been used, might equally well have been. Horatius Bonar, Reginald Heber and Mrs. Alexander are typical authors of this kind—not to mention the enormously prolific Wesley and Watts. The body of their work is hymnody, whether ever sung or not, as much as Fanny Crosby's—not a verse of whose vast output, probably, failed to find music and singers. In this class it is intention which counts. Then we have also included in full such poems as sections of Keble's *The Christian Year* which, not written with the hymn-book in mind, have nevertheless with a little adjustment proved eminently adaptable to it, and indeed almost unthinkable outside it. Here it has been the proof of long practice which has become decisive: the congregational voice has transmuted poem into hymn.

Singing is the root of the matter where the hymn is concerned. It is as song that we first meet the hymn; and for vast numbers of us participation in hymn-singing is our most intimate contact with music. We first become acquainted with them at school; and the whole body of English-speaking church-goers sings several hymns every Sunday at least. For the great majority of people today, there is no other form of music-making which enters more closely into their lives. To all intents and purposes the folk-song and the ballad have disappeared. The modern popular song may sell in terms of thousands of gramophone records, or even sheets of music, be heard by countless cinema-goers, radio-listeners or television-viewers, but it is not sung by them to any notable extent. Much of the time, indeed, a piece of today's popular music is not basically a song so much as a length of dance-music with supplementary words

2

attached. The words are at best a vehicle for the tune. Hymns, on the other hand, are only practicable as songs.

But the hymn is at the same time a poem, though this point can be obscured by the fact that it is sung. Important as its musical aspect may be, the whole point of the hymn lies in its words—otherwise it is a mere interlude of entertainment. And just as the hymn provides the most important personal contact of many people with song, so it provides them with their most important contact with poetry. In many cases it is their only contact with poetry, to which they may give not a single thought during the other six days of the week.

Hymns are therefore, for incalculable numbers of people, an intensely formative influence on their taste in poetry—even though it is one which may later be rejected, consciously or unconsciously. For others, hymns may provide their only experience of the art—but none the less a cherished experience. It is certainly true that early acquaintance alone means that lines from hymns keep a tenacious grip on the mind, so making it easy to receive lines from them as proverbial—such lines of Watts as,

"How doth the little busy bee improve each shining hour".

A sure proof of their universal acceptance is that hymns are often parodied, or have secular words fitted to their tunes: for instance W. P. Mackay's hymn,

"We praise thee, O God! for the Son of thy love"

is obviously the prototype of the famous satirical song of the International Workers of the World which begins,

"Oh, why don't you work, like other men do?"

Other hymns are often used by large gatherings of people assembled for non-religious occasions as community songs, absolutely spontaneously and unselfconsciously: to take a familiar example, "Abide with Me" is a particular favourite with football crowds.

3

Hymns are, in fact, with their general familiarity and their detachment from the ups and downs of fashionable favour, not only the nearest approach we now have to a permanent popular song, but the nearest approach to a popular literature.

Popular literature, however, while it is truly such, always suffers from a peculiar disadvantage. It is not looked upon as literature by those in whose lives it figures, and it is disregarded by those with formally "literary" interests. To those who sing hymns the main point is that they are an act of devotion, and this isolates them for those who consider poetry an esoteric art practised only by a chosen group of immortals. In how many anthologies do Watts, Wesley or Heber figure as even minor poets?

The purpose of this book is to put the hymn in English into its proper place in English poetry—for a poem it always is, and often a poem at an astonishingly high level. It is also not genre poetry, any more than Renaissance religious art is genre painting. The range of emotion, subject and imagery included in the body of English hymnody is by no means limited.

Because they have been neglected many hymn-writers have slipped, as we have said, into a false anonymity; and yet their influence on poets whose names are in every text-book is indisputable. In the manner of the time, Blake's childhood education in poetry must have been haunted as much, if not more, by Watts as by Shakespeare; and that he was profoundly conscious of Whitefield and Wesley is plain from the reference to them in *Milton*:

"Can you have greater miracles than these? Men who devote
    Their life's whole comfort to intire scorn & injury & death?"

He can hardly have known the men without knowing their hymns. The *Songs of Innocence and of Experience* at times have a flavour of Watts or Newton or Wesley struck with genius.

Emily Brontë, not so many years later, must have known hymns intimately in her father's parsonage: and that she knew

—and despised— the hymnody of dissent is evident from her treatment of Joseph in *Wuthering Heights*. The influences on her poetry were no doubt manifold; but not only the metre but the diction itself of the eighteenth-century hymn-writers can be traced in such lines as these:

> "Then let thy bleeding branch atone
>   For every torturing fear:
> Shall my young sins, my sins alone,
>   Be everlasting here?"

The influence of hymns upon poets is one which has decreased: but A. E. Housman himself is the witness to how they affected him. Not only the metric range of his own poetry testifies to this, but his remark in *The Name and Nature of Poetry*:

"'It is surely superfluous,' says Johnson, 'to answer the question that has once been asked, whether Pope was a poet, otherwise than by asking in return, if Pope be not a poet, where is poetry to be found?' It is to be found, Dr. Johnson, in Dr. Watts."

When one comes to discuss the qualities of the actual hymns, two standards immediately present themselves. Countless thousands of hymns are in existence, and it is perfectly true that from the literary point of view the vast majority are worthless—a stricture which applies to every known branch of literature, from the epic to the science-fiction story. But because hymns are essentially functional they are perfectly capable of fulfilling their function, and thus of being technically excellent hymns, without having a grain of literary grace in a single line. Such hymns will be applauded by hymnologists, with perfect justice; but not by the editors of this anthology. No doctrinal stand of any kind is taken in this book; the hymns in it have been selected entirely because they are beautiful or striking in one way or another—and in how many ways Christian writers have achieved these effects can perhaps only be seen in reading it.

It can be said, with perfect truth, that the qualities so brilliantly deployed by many of these hymn-writers are matched, even surpassed, by other poets who are already better known. Vigour, tenderness, profundity, colour, charm—all these we know already. But where hymns have never been equalled is in the effects they have been able to extort from the limitations of their chosen form. Simplicity—not necessarily austerity—is essential to the hymn, imposed inevitably by its function; and no other body of poetry in the English language has distilled such richness from simplicity.

The paucity of the few metres used by hymn-writers until about 1820, under the dominance of the tunes in common use and the spareness of the language they felt bound to adopt, resulted in a curious effect. It consists of a strong sense of reality and conviction, a vitality, even when the poet is employing ideas and images which have been employed a thousand times before, and will be used a thousand times again. Because his words are so simple, indeed, and his stock of subjects so familiar, the least variation on them has a singular force. Take for instance Seagrave's *Drawing*: there is not an original thought in it, not an image that was not a commonplace. But their juxtaposition as Seagrave brought them together gives the poem an almost surrealist force. It is a process which operates right down to individual words. In Wesley's hymn for condemned criminals, the grave verses are suddenly heightened by the extraordinary phrase "Me and my dying mates." The touch of bad grammar, the touch of slang, are lightly applied: but they are exactly all that are needed to give the hymn a severe and colloquial power. Such strokes are not applied with coyness or deliberate artifice: they are never, in these hymns, contrived; but where they occur they bring to the reader a new sense of the value of individual words, no matter how well-worn. In this way, properly read, these hymns give us a renewed insight into our language: and to do so is one of the most valuable offices of poetry.

6

The authors of these hymns are an interesting body of men and women. They had hardly one thing in common with each other except the love of God that they expressed in poetry. Few of them indeed were professed poets: or if, early in life, they had literary ambitions, they soon sank them in what they considered greater aims. Foremost among these, naturally, stood the religious life: and the majority of our hymn-writers pursued it, whether as country parsons, missionaries, theologians, travelling preachers, deans, canons, bishops, or laymen suffused with the love of God. They were Roman Catholics, Anglicans, Baptists, Methodists, Moravians, Muggletonians—members of a score of shades of belief about the Christian religion. But they also included journalists, educationalists, an ex-slave-trader, a doctor, courtiers, novelists, politicians, statesmen, an ex-coal-miner—people of every kind of trade and at every social level.

That such a heterogeneous assemblage should have practised the art of hymn-writing and have practised it with such admirable results, is a fresh proof—if any proof is needed—of the natural bent of English-speaking people towards poetry as a means of emotional expression. Not in any one period alone, but in all of them, it seems to have been possible for almost anyone to write at least one good poem in a lifetime. Many have chosen to make that one a hymn. Hence the writers who are represented here by one excellent hymn and nothing more: only too often they wrote numerous others which are quite valueless.

The hymn-writers have had an advantage not possessed by any schools of poetry contemporary with them. They have been able to draw—indeed they have almost been obliged to draw—upon one of the richest storehouses of imagery in existence: the Bible. The strong thread of images derived from both the Old and the New Testaments—the stock of glittering pictures of deserts and oriental courts from Israelite history, the symbols of parable and Passion from the life of Jesus, the fantastic visions of the Apocalypse—all these are for the hymn-writer an unparalleled mine open to his hand. He has used it unhesitatingly and unsparingly; and he has automatically gained thereby for his work a pictorial splendour which, though to some extent ready-made, is none the less powerful in its effect. Ready-made too, to a certain extent, is his language, for (again perfectly legitimately) he has often taken over wholesale the very words of the Bible for his use. The process may be compared to the variations on someone else's theme which composers have frequently written; while the power of the biblical words gives the work of lesser poets an authority it could probably never attain otherwise.

The limitations of space alone preclude any possibility of our giving anything like a detailed history of hymn-writing. But hymn-writing during the last four hundred years does fall naturally into several periods, and it will be helpful to define these.

ROMAN CATHOLIC AND CHURCH OF ENGLAND. 1560–1655

At the time of the Reformation, the English Church had the alternatives of Lutheranism or Calvinism before it; by choosing Calvinism it defined the path which the history of the hymn was to follow. Luther, deeply attached as he personally was to singing, bequeathed his followers a valued legacy of hymns: but in the eyes of Calvinists these were an unnecessary, even an unlawful, addition to the canonical texts of Christianity and could only end in competing with the Psalms. It was therefore only by way of the Psalms that hymns could develop as authorised parts of the service; a process which took a couple of centuries to complete.

Several translations of the Psalms were made at an early date. The French translations of Clement Marot, printed at Geneva in 1562, were the inspiration of the Psalter of Sternhold and Hopkins, which drew on the translations William Kethe had published the previous year. "Sternhold and Hopkins" or the "Old Psalter" soon became the standard work used in English churches, holding its own against several later comers. From it has been drawn one of the most stately of all hymns: "All people that on earth do dwell" (often familiarly called "The Old Hundredth" after its source the hundreth Psalm) a splendid example of Tudor verse at its best.

Unofficially, many poems called "hymns" were written over the next hundred years or so, but the description was used in what we should now consider a somewhat loose way. Some of these may have been written for congregational singing or may not, but were so used at the time. Donne's hymn is a case in point. The sacred poems of Thomas Campion were published in part-settings, and must have been sung by small private groups of people as acts of devotion—the same is true of some of George Herbert's poems. Others, whatever fate their authors intended for them, have been successfully put into commission as congregational hymns at various times since. But at the time, any such use of a poem, no matter how it was described at the top of the page, was distinctly unorthodox.

SCOTLAND AND DISSENTERS. 1578–1697

Early hymnody made its best progress among the early dissenters. The songs of the three Wedderburn brothers are an interesting link between the old and new religions, the ballads and hymnody. These were published in broadsheet form about 1542, and first collected into a book some fifteen years later. Their tone is often truculent and clearly political: it comes as no surprise to learn that James and John Wedderburn were arraigned, persecuted, and exiled for heresy about 1540. Many of their songs are translations from the German—are these by John, who fled to Wittemberg?—but those included here are from English originals. "Quho is at my windo, quho?" is based on a ballad whose opening line in the version given in Beaumont and Fletcher's *Knight of the Burning*

Pestle is "Go from my window, love, go." The tune of "With huntis up" was known as early as 1537, but the words usually given are said to have been written by a man called Gray; the first verse of the ballad ascribed to him is:

> "The hunt is up, the hunt is up,
> And it is well nigh day
> And Harry our king is gone hunting
> To bring his deer to bay."

Wither's hymns have been somewhat swamped by the average mediocrity of his work and its enormous quantity—from 1612 to the end of his days hardly twelve months passed without his publishing some book or pamphlet. *Haleluiah* was issued during the Civil War, even that tremendous event failing to curtail Wither's literary activities particularly. This in spite of the fact that he served at first for the King against the Covenanters then, with greater conviction, entered the Puritan army with the rank of captain. On one occasion he was captured by the royalists and only saved by a plea by Sir John Denham that he should be spared on the grounds that while Wither lived, Denham could not be called the worst poet in England. Wither resented this more than was reasonable, all things considered; but while it was a useful joke, it was certainly not entirely justified.

Wither was the first man to attempt a comprehensive body of hymns; like his nonconformist successors generally, he compiled his book in terms of occasions rather than according to the festivals of the church, which the dissenters disliked. Wither was curiously fitted by temperament to do this. His sympathetic nature entered into the circumstances of which he wrote fully and with charity. He did not take animals or the deformed as the mere objects for sermonising, as many of his contemporaries would have done; he wrote as far as possible, and very touchingly, from the point of view of either.

The abounding self-consciousness of the Commonwealth, however, found perhaps more popular expression in topical hymns. These were quite often composed by clergymen for the use of their congregations: as for example the hymns written to celebrate Cromwell's victory at Musselburgh in 1650 "by those three reverend, and learned Divines, Mr. John Goodwin, Mr. Dasoser Powel and Mr. Appletree sung in their respective congregations." The best hymn of this kind is William Barton's hymn on Naseby, which is also a good specimen of Barton's voluminous body of work. In spite of his frequent and somewhat imprecise complaints about enemies who were hindering him, Barton succeeded in becoming a figure of great significance in the development of hymnody. His first *Century of Select Hymns* was published in 1659, and he wrote others assiduously until this book was expanded to the *Six Centuries* published by his son in 1688. He supported his work with the precedents of the Apostles, the early Church and the Bohemian Brethren (who were later to make their peculiar contribution to hymnody as the Moravians). He insisted that hymns must be firmly founded on the Scriptures. Accordingly his own, perhaps the earliest of true English congregational hymns, consist of collections of quatrains, each based on a biblical text, the reference for which stands at its head. Unoriginal compilations as they mostly are, Barton secured for them by this method a certain measure of divine authority. Consequently Barton's, rather than Wither's, course was the one that hymn-writing followed for many years to come.

The more extreme branches of dissent looked upon hymn-singing with horror. It was laid down in 1608 by John Smyth, the founder of Baptism, that the New Covenant was spiritual, from the heart, and that reading—singing also therefore—was a sin. This dictum was eventually challenged by Benjamin Keach, who launched upon the Baptist movement his belief that congregational song was ordained by Christ, and was perfectly prepared to argue forever that he was right. There was something a little cracked about Keach, a strange man who gives the impression of being half-illiterate, half-genius. He pegged away at the great "Controversie of Singing", stirred up by himself, all through the closing years of the seventeenth century; the upshot of it was that Baptists were permitted to sing or not as they wished.

CHURCH OF ENGLAND. 1683–1712

Meanwhile the position of hymns in the Church of England remained undecided. Private hymn-singing appears to have been practised sporadically; Bishop Ken wrote his magnificent hymns for his scholars at Winchester College. The first person in the Church of England to write what were intended to be hymns for congregational singing was apparently John Mason. He was a haunted, neurotic man; the influence which George Herbert's poems is said to have had on him found ample scope for effect in his character. His agonies of penitence have behind them the force of a singleness of mind which is far more impressive than the vacillations of others, such as Hammond, who followed the same trains of thought in later years. But Mason's work was irresistibly, with its personal stresses, nearer to the spirit of dissent than to his own church; and no other hymns of importance by its members were written for years until the trial pieces, correct and Augustan, of Joseph Addison.

The Church of England's official variety of sacred song was still the Psalm. Most of its members had no objection to this, but many had lost their respect for Sternhold and Hopkins. A version was therefore set in hand by Nahum Tate in collaboration with Nicholas Brady. Tate had had a successful literary career; among other activities he rewrote Shakespeare liberally, *Richard II* becoming *The Sicilian Usurper* under his touch, while he had relieved the end of *Lear* of its gloom by allowing Cordelia to get off scot-free and marry Edmund. In 1692, upon the death of Shadwell, he was appointed poet laureate—the worst of poets laureate with the exception of his predecessor, it has been said: but that was by Southey. The truth seems to be that Tate was a quiet, amiable man with a weakness for drink; and he was intelligent enough to be esteemed by Purcell and Dryden. Brady, an Irishman like Tate, was an extremely popular preacher who was chaplain first to William III and later to Anne. Their version of the Psalter was probably the best work that either of them did. The first announcement of it appeared in 1695, and the whole book was published in the following year as *A New Version of the Psalms of David*.

A supplement followed a few years later containing sixteen versified passages from Scripture, including the Commandments, the *Te Deum, Benedictus, Veni Creator, Magnificat* and *Nunc Dimittis*. Which author was responsible for any one part of the book is impossible to settle. It is believed that Tate wrote the more poetical psalms—"As pants the hart" and "While shepherds watched" are generally believed to be his—and it is conceivable that Dryden helped him with them.

The *New Version* was dedicated to the Sovereign, and shortly after its publication was "Allowed" by the King in Council "to be used in all Churches, Chappells and Congregations, as shall think fit to receive the same"; it was also commended by the Archbishop of Canterbury and the Bishop of London. Nevertheless, "Tate and Brady" met with determined opposition from the conservative. It was accused of being inaccurate, "modish", "fashionable" and even "gay". These objections —felt strongly by many—militated against its ever being universally acceptable. In a great part of the country, indeed, it sank without a trace; London, however, received it more gratefully. But whatever its defects, the book's form, its tone, and its literary quality were such as to accustom members of the Church generally to the possibility of singing actual hymns.

ISAAC WATTS AND HIS FOLLOWERS. 1709–1787

There can be no doubt at all that many conscientious members of the clergy at this time were disgusted by the state of psalm-singing in their churches; but they were at a loss to know what could be done to remedy matters. For these Isaac Watts, an Independent, was the spokesman: he examined what was actually done, he worked out what should be done and then set about doing it. The story is that when he was about eighteen he spoke disparagingly of one of the versified psalms sung in his father's church, only to be challenged, "Give us something which will be better, young man". Watts thereupon wrote his first hymn, and it was sung at the following evening service. He continued to write hymns until he was the only talented writer up to that time who had studied the problems involved, not with passion nor with, necessarily, inspiration: but with systematic attention to technique.

Congregational singing at that time must certainly have been deplorable. It was customary to sing six verses from the psalm, pretty well regardless of continuity or even sense. Nobody took psalm-books to church with them, except the parish clerk, who led the congregation by the curious method known as "lining-out". He would read out the psalm a line at a time, to be followed by the congregation singing it in unison; he would then proceed to the next line, the congregation would repeat that after him, and so on till the end. Every one in church certainly had to concentrate to know what he was singing: but the disadvantages of the practice were quite peculiar to it. In the first place, the clerk's position was often bestowed on him as a form of charity, which did not make for a high standard of clerkly intelligence: these men were perfectly capable of dropping out a line or a verse here, there or anywhere exactly as they felt disposed. No musical direction was given, so that the singing itself was chaotic. It was also astonishingly leisurely; every note was dragged out to expiration point, so that it had been known for a vicar who had left his sermon behind, to announce a psalm, walk half a mile home and back, and return to find his flock still deeply occupied with the words of David. All this led with the best will in the world, to a certain lassitude on the part of the singers. It is no wonder that Watts, faced week by week with this travesty, wrote:

"While we sing the Praises of our God in his Church, we are employ'd in that part of Worship which of all others is the nearest a-kin to Heaven; and 'tis pity that this of all others should be perform'd the worst upon Earth . . . To see the dull Indifference, the negligent and the thoughtless Air that sits upon the Faces of a whole Assembly, while the Psalm is on their lips, might tempt even a charitable Observer to suspect the Fervency of inward Religion."*

However, Watts believed that it was not merely the manner of singing that was obstructive, it was often the matter itself. He thought it distracting for an English congregation of the early eighteenth century, in the midst of praising the Lord, suddenly to have placed before it the personal preoccupations of the Psalmist: and then, he said, "our Consciences are affrighted lest we should speak a Falsehood unto God." Watts therefore, while like his forerunners he often adhered closely to biblical texts, wrote hymns which were intended to be a direct expression of the worshippers' feelings—for it was one of his firmest tenets that the congregation's song should represent the Christian's address to his God; while the Psalm should be read as part of the Word of the Lord.

With considerable realism Watts accepted "lining-out" as inevitable, although he evidently disliked "the unhappy Mixture of Reading and Singing, which cannot presently be reformed". Accordingly, he said, he seldom put a stop into the middle of a line, or left an end lacking one. He kept his language as plain as possible. He used four metres, and saw that each verse could be fitted to the best-known and most commonly used tunes. He did all he could to ensure that his work was simple and practical, even when he felt that in the process he was making it too simple, too unliterary, to be considered the poetry for which he knew he had the talent. That he did not care for this he made abundantly clear: his purpose was to write singable hymns, and his poetry could take its chances so long as he succeeded at that.

* Preface to *Hymns and Spiritual Songs*.

As it turned out, he did succeed on both grounds, though it is obvious that both his strictly poetic talent and his personal instincts were to some extent trampled upon in his determination that nothing should stand between him and his God. Watts was a warm, tender-hearted man with a particular love of children, as his *Divine Songs* show: but one also sees, in his touching poem *The Hazard of loving the Creatures*, how even so natural and kindly an instinct presented itself to him as a falling short from a higher duty. It was a painful struggle to an evidently lonely man; but it was the amalgam, worked by his single-mindedness, of poetic and personal renunciation that resulted in such poems of intense longing as *God invisible, A prospect of Heaven*, and *A Sight of God*. Its culmination is, perhaps, one of the most famous of all hymns: *Crucifixion to the World*—"When I survey the wondrous Cross". This splendid poem, so sober in its antitheses, so grave in its quiet movement, brings calm and dignity to the eighteenth-century poem of wit. Here Watts incidentally made one of the most important changes from the first edition of his book, in the revised fifth edition from which our versions are taken. The second line originally was the beautiful

> "Where the young Prince of Glory dy'd."

Pursuant to his aim of regularity for the sake of the singer, Watts established the iambics firmly in the better-known

> "On which the Prince of Glory dy'd."

—abandoning a touch of sentiment, perhaps, but perfecting the verse's dignity. Nevertheless, the hint of sentiment recalls, like the third verse, that Watts was after all a baroque writer—a fact which also suddenly emerges in the description, at once charming and disconcerting, like a minor contemporary German or Spanish religious painting, of how the Eternal

> "Rides on a Cloud disdainful by
> A *Sultan* or a *Czar*."

This unexpected quality appears often in Watts' versions of the Psalms, which, Christianised and Anglicised according to Watts' lights, at moments appear almost as the occasional poems of a patriotic Briton. At the same time the book contains what may be considered Watts' masterpiece, "Our God, our help in ages past", which he never surpassed in grandeur, and which few other hymn-writers have equalled.

After speaking of Watts' finest hymns, it is not ungrateful to admit that many of them are weak. This fact, however, did not affect his enormous success in the effort he was making—to put decent hymns in the mouths of English-speaking congregations. His own were greeted at once with pleasure and emotion: country congregations were known to weep during the singing of them. *Divine Songs* became a nursery classic; for many devout adults the *Hymns* and *Psalms* were daily reading. Nor was this a temporary fervour. The hymns of Watts were pre-eminently the hymns of English-speaking Christianity to many for a hundred years; stories are told of people who refused to sing any others, and silently sat tight in their seats when others were announced.

In spite of this general acceptance, Watts' example naturally inspired individual followers—his friend Doddridge is one, and probably the best. His posthumous book, edited inaccurately by his friend Job Orton in 1755,* was introduced to many congregations as a supplement to the hymn-book of Watts.

In time, of course, collections were published, usually under the rather mock-modest title of "Supplements to Watts". Of these one of the most important and best was John Rippon's *A selection of Hymns from the Best Authors, intended to be an Appendix to Dr. Watts's Psalms and Hymns* (1787). It ran into a number of successively enlarged editions, some of them made by other hands after his death. Rippon's *Selection* included the first appearance of the anonymous and monumental hymn "How

---

* Our versions are derived from the edition, corrected from Doddridge's manuscripts, published by his great-grandson in 1839.

firm a foundation"—surely, with its Handelian sonority, written long before its date of publication.

MINOR SECTS, PART I. 1726–1754

Many minor sects were in existence at the same time, such as that of David Culy and his Culimites who lived in Essex—always fruitful ground for sectarian eccentricity—and held beliefs similar to those of the Anabaptists. But the most important contribution these groups made to hymnody was through the extraordinary episode of the Moravians in England, which was to affect in some degree the development of the hymn.

The Moravians represented a revival of the doctrines of John Hus, who is said to have originated the practice of hymn-singing for his Bohemian Brethren. In 1722 a travelling preacher called Christian David led a refugee band of the Brethren out of Moravia, and was given refuge by the mystically-minded Count Zinzendorf. After the settlement had been in existence some years, Zinzendorf became one of its members in faith. He had always been addicted to founding brotherhoods with such names as "The Slaves of Virtue" and "The Honourable Order of the Mustard Seed"; now, at Herrnhut, he inaugurated "The Order of the Little Fools", basing on Matthew xi.25 his contention that the Moravians should be as like babes as possible. This led to the "Sifting-time" of 1743–1750, the period of extraordinary imagery during which the Moravians referred to Christ as "Brother Lambkin", the Count as "Little Papa", and themselves as little wound-parsons, little cross-wood splinters, and joyous little wound-worms. When Zinzendorf came to his senses, he reformed the Church on new standards of sobriety, so that it was on a firmer basis than ever at his death in 1760.

Two notable aspects of the sect were its devotion to missionary work and to hymn-singing. Their first important contact with English religious life occurred in 1735, when a party of Moravian colonists crossed the Atlantic with John and Charles

Wesley and Benjamin Ingham. The English were bound for Georgia as missionaries; and John Wesley in particular was deeply moved by the unforced enthusiasm of the Germans' hymn-singing, recognising it as what he would wish to hear from congregations at home.

On his return from America he entered into close contact with the London Moravians; but a serious breach opened in 1740. When the extravagance of the "Sifting-time" spread to England, Wesley was horrified to discover that he had been so closely associated with, that he had drawn inspiration from, people who could write about sacred matters with a combination of baby-talk and graphic physical detail.

The Moravian hymns are memorable, if for no other reason than that there can be little else like them in the English language. In their diminutives and their preoccupation with wounds, they are intensely Germanic: one might almost be standing in the midst of some collection of Crucifixions or Pietas from Rococo churches, with their inimitable blending of the horror of neat incisions and of nursery cosiness.

CHARLES WESLEY: HIS CONTEMPORARIES AND FOLLOWERS.
1739–1798

John Wesley himself, compared to his brother Charles, wrote few hymns. At one time it was believed he was the author of less than forty—a drop in the bucket compared to Charles's vast output of some seven thousand. It is now believed, however, that his share of the work was somewhat greater.

The Church of England—which still clung to Sternhold and Hopkins, and Tate and Brady—still looked upon hymns distrustfully. When he finally broke away from it, John Wesley followed the lesson of the Moravians and his own instincts to make singing a staple of the Methodist service. He himself regulated the character of the music, noting that it should be sung briskly, heartily, in time, and above all with reverent attention. "Why should the devil have all the good tunes?"

was his famous question. Charles, in a hymn of 1749, expressed the same thought:

> "Listed into the cause of sin,
>   Why should a good be evil?
> Music, alas, too long has been
>   Press'd to obey the devil.

> "He that a sprinkled conscience hath,
>   He that in God is merry,
> Let him sing psalms, the Spirit saith,
>   Joyful, and never weary,
> Offer the sacrifice of praise,
>   Hearty, and never ceasing,
> Spiritual songs and anthems raise
>   Honour, and thanks, and blessing."

But he did not neglect to draw the contrasting picture in a pendent hymn:

> "The Drunkards proclaim
>   At midnight their shame,
>   Their sacrifice bring,
> And loud to the praise of *their* master they sing.
>   The hellish desires,
>   Which Satan inspires,
>   In sonnets they breathe,
> And shouting descend to the mansion of death.

> "The civiller crowd,
>   In theatres proud,
>   Acknowledge his power,
> And Satan in nightly assemblies adore:
>   To the masque and the ball
>   They fly at his call;
>   Or in pleasures excel,
> And chant in a grove* to the harpers of hell.

* "Ranelagh Gardens, Vauxhall, etc."

20

> "Our concert of praise
> To Jesus we raise
> And all the night long
> Continue the new evangelical song:
> We dance to the fame
> Of Jesus's name,
> The joy it imparts
> Is heaven begun in our musical hearts."

John spent much time criticising hymns remorselessly, whether they were by Charles or anyone else, and compiling hymn-books for his followers. Over fifty of these were issued during the Wesleys' lifetimes, but the most important was the great *Collection of Hymns for the Use of the People called Methodists*, published in 1780. This was the foundation of Methodist hymnody.

The character of Charles Wesley's hymns was unlike anything seen so far. It has been said of them that they introduced in English hymnody its special theological tone, but this is to put the matter coldly. Shaken with the prospect of salvation as an inexpressibly wonderful gift bestowed upon the entire human race, Wesley writes in joy and rapture of this revelation. Nothing is too great or too small to be celebrated. A large proportion of his hymns is occasional, because every occasion shone in the light of God's grace. He begins many hymns "And . . ." or "But . . ." as though breaking from silence into the full spate of pent-up speech. Metrically he is more able, was more complex, than any hymn-writer to this time; a legacy perhaps from the days of Moravian influence as much as his brother's introduction of new tunes. He has a broad humanity, and can speak as though from the mouths of the brutalised colliers, who flocked around his brother, without condescension; or as from a condemned murderer, without repulsion. His are the hymns of a great man, if not uniformly those of a great poet.

Wesley's hymns, during his own long life, provided an

impetus to many other writers of different denominations. None of them was as great a man, though some now and again wrote finer poems than he had done. It had, however, become an age for the compilation of hymn-books, both those which followed after Watts and those which followed after Wesley. Not that they were mutually exclusive: a common stock of hymns was accumulating into which all dipped at will—thus, incidentally, establishing that practice of tinkering by editors which the Wesleys disapproved of being applied to their own work, although they exercised it on others'.

But it was also a period when hymn-books were being written. The most famous today is the *Olney Hymns* of John Newton and William Cowper. The lives of these two men form a curious contrast. Cowper, in spite of his melancholia and his madness, was essentially a literary man and a scholar bound by nature to his study. Newton's early life was a picaresque affair: he spent years at sea in the merchant service and the slave trade, suffering hardship and shipwreck as almost daily incidents. After the storm in which he suddenly became aware of his sinfulness, as the ship limped homeward its captain was half-inclined to look upon Newton as a Jonah who should be tossed overboard; and Newton was half-inclined to agree with him. When after the subsequent years of effort and study he obtained his ordination, the burly man who always insisted on wearing an old sea-jacket became recognised as one of the finest preachers of his time.

Cowper came to Olney, Newton's parish, in 1767, and in 1771 the two planned their collaboration. Cowper contributed altogether sixty-seven hymns—some of which he had had in hand since 1764—before his part of the work was terminated by an attack of madness in 1773. It is said that "God moves in a mysterious way" was his response to the intimation that his brain was giving way. Newton continued the work, and the remaining 281 Olney hymns are his.

Fragmentary, though in parts fine, as Cowper's madness made his connection with the book, it is Newton's contribution which stands out today. They are quite distinguishable—Cowper's delicate, introverted verse against Newton's thumping metres and forthright positiveness. The old sea-captain turned preacher shows time after time a solid power of producing firm, strong poems; and no other hymn-writer has used so convincingly imagery drawn from animals and the earth.

All these were evangelical manifestations, and as such distrusted by the Church of England. Nevertheless, there were hymn-writers in the Church; among them was A. M. Toplady, who in some obscure way, almost as a side-issue in his guerilla warfare with Wesley, wrote perhaps the most famous hymn of all—"Rock of Ages". A hymn-book for the Church, although it was not universally accepted, was actually compiled by the Rev. Martin Madan, who later fell into a certain disrepute as a result of his writing a treatise advocating polygamy.

MINOR SECTS, PART II. 1757–1794

Anyone who still clings to a conception of the eighteenth century as an intellectual age of wit-minded atheists is invited to contemplate the period's minor sects. Perhaps at no other time did more eccentric interpreters of the Christian religion not merely spring into the light, but gain active groups of followers.

A new generation of Muggletonians was in full strength, carrying on the beliefs bequeathed to them by Muggleton and Reeve years before. Very curious beliefs they were: the early lives of Lodowick Muggleton (1609–1698) and John Reeve (1608–1658) were undistinguished until Reeve announced that Christ had appointed him the messenger of a new order, and that Muggleton was to be his spokesman. Subsequently they taught that normally God has no interest in human affairs, with such rare exceptions as the commission to Reeve; that Reeve was Moses and Muggleton was Aaron; together with such vulnerable contentions as that heaven is six miles above the earth. There were such groups as the Inghamites, offshoots of the Moravians; there were also secessionists from the established church, such as the Glassites, later the Sandemanians. Most of these were politically radical, refusing to acknowledge the recognised religions or civil authorities, and running into the difficulties which might be anticipated. All of them naturally had their own poets who produced hymns consonant with their specialised beliefs.

THE NINETEENTH CENTURY. 1820–1908

At the outset of the nineteenth century, in the midst of several flourishing schools of hymn-writers, the Church of England's official attitude was still wary and distrustful. As late as 1819 a Sheffield vicar was summoned to the York Diocesan Court to answer for his use of a hymn-book compiled by himself and his organist. The tide of disfavour was turning, however; the Archbishop desired the book to be withdrawn, but authorised and paid for a revised edition to be published in the following year.

Both these actions—the prosecution and the permission granted—were indicative of the way the wind was blowing. The Church of England recognised its need for a hymn-book it could approve: the question was where it could be found. The case of Reginald Heber proved typical. Heber was one of the last romantics. As a child he was a prodigy who translated the *Phaedrus* into English verse before he was seven. At Oxford he won the University Prize for Latin verse in his first year, a triumph which he followed by winning the Newdigate Prize with his poem on *Palestine* in 1803. This was a success which reached far beyond Oxford, for the poem—now almost forgotten—became one of the best-known of the first half of the century. On taking his degree Heber was at once elected a Fellow of All Souls, and set out on a long tour through Scandinavia and Russia. Fourteen years at the family living of Hodnet followed; then, in 1822, he was offered the Bishopric of Calcutta. After hesitating for a while, he accepted the enormous burden: his duties extended not only over the whole sub-continent, but over Ceylon and Australasia. The work had killed Heber's predecessor; in 1826 it killed him.

While he was at Hodnet, Heber felt acutely the need for a good hymnal. Temporarily he installed the *Olney Hymns* for the use of his parishioners, and meanwhile worked steadily at the compilation of a book himself. He called in contributions from his literary friends—Scott, whom he had known at Oxford, and H. H. Milman; he chose suitable hymns by older writers; and he arranged them for liturgical use. When Heber's *Hymns* was published posthumously in 1827, its practicality and poetic worth dissipated most of the doubts about the value of hymns that still persisted. Heber himself, an intensely literate man, who had been hailed at Oxford as one of England's most promising young poets, could not be shrugged off as a mere enthusiastic evangelical. The hymns were in an easily recognisable contemporary idiom—exotic and lavish in imagery, passionate in feeling. They were, in fact, in the vein of Thomas Moore and his master Byron. The Church of England's great objection to hymns as the work of the individual writer was based on the overwhelming consciousness of self displayed by Wesley, by Newton and Cowper, even by Watts. Heber's were neither amorously or impertinently personal, as he was at pains to indicate, obviously with the Moravians and their like in mind. No hymns show more than his a detached but vibrant exaltation at the thought of the splendours of Heaven, at the glory of the Lord's wrath. They have in them the riches of the Orient as Heber pictured it when, as a child, he would trace imaginary journeys across the map of that India which he had no idea he would ever see.

What Heber did for the hymn-book, as distinct from the hymn, was to systematise its modern form. Whereas the hymn-book had so far been, for the Church of England, either a non-conformist song-book or a supplement to the Psalms, Heber's arrangement of hymns for Sundays and Festivals gave it a new standing as an adjunct of the Prayer Book.

Here, it seemed, was a corrective to the great school of hymn-writers which had been growing up for thirty years. Innumerable magazines, gift-books, remembrancers, keepsakes, and other such ephemerides had been printing hymns by private people during that period. Hymn-writing had become a natural means of expression for devout people, just as hymn-singing was a popular religious exercise for the evening in the increasingly domestic life of the nineteenth century. But within a very few years Heber's effort was to diminish in comparison with another and a greater. Six years after his death, the Oxford Movement began its explosive course with the leadership of Newman, Pusey and John Keble, a movement motivated by a belief that the Church had drifted too far into Protestantism, and needed to be recalled to its ancient but obscured principles. The first step to the accomplishment of this was the publication of the famous series of *Tracts for the Times*. Certain of the Movement's followers were seized with such a sense of revision indeed that some of them—F. W. Faber, Edward Caswall and Newman himself—found themselves in the Roman Catholic Church.

But a natural consequence of the Oxford Movement's concern with ancient forms of the Church was a series of explorations into its Latin and Greek repertoire of hymns. First Isaac Williams, then John Chandler made researches and translations; a little later came J. M. Neale, perhaps the most learned and certainly the most thorough of all. Neale is one of the best known of hymn-writers; he is perhaps better known than he deserves. For many people, Christmas is inextricably associated with "Good King Wenceslas", which is one of Neale's translations; nevertheless it is actually a rather banal piece of verse, nowhere near the standard of his best work. This appeared in a long series of books and pamphlets, some of them addressed to "Children", "The Manufacturers", and "the People". Neale's reactionary political beliefs caused him to have some difficulty in striking the right chord to suit the two latter classes, which were sometimes provoked to unsympathetic rejections. Neale did not have an original mind; he is rarely powerful, nor has he a great deal of feeling; his early *Hymns for the Sick* (1843) represent his limit in certain directions. He had, however, an intensely aesthetic sensibility which allowed him to revel in the implied pageantry of much biblical and ecclesiastical imagery just as Heber did; but without Heber's fire. In the hands of such an accomplished craftsman, the outcome was the production of a large body of very beautiful hymns. They certainly influenced a number of other hymn-writers; Gerard Moultrie, for instance, whose extraordinary work shows the effects of Neale—also, one would guess, that of William Morris's early poems.

Side by side with this kind of hymnody there ran many others. They include hymns for all sorts of people and occasions, joyful or sad. It is surprising how often there emerges a poet as good and little-known as J. D. Burns, for example, with his strong and sombre *The footsteps of the flock*, or as Henry Twells with his well-known "At even ere the sun was set".

Most of these writers, it is true, were restricted in their range; one of the least constrained was Mrs. C. F. Alexander. Her hymns for children and adults have a remarkable scope. In mood, manner and subject they include the simple, the passionate, and the grand. She is one of the best of the English hymn-writers, and has a strong claim to be the best nineteenth-century hymn-writer after Heber. Strictly as a hymn-writer indeed, she might be called superior to him; but she was not as good a poet as he when she wrote *St. Mark the Evangelist*, any more than she was as simple and tender as Watts in her *Hymns for Children*; or as anguished as Cowper in "When wounded sore the stricken soul". But still all these are fine poems. They are, besides, evidence that while unlike most of her contemporaries she attempted a great deal, to a surprising degree her efforts were successful. The total impression left by her work is a rich one.

Following Heber, several of these writers arranged their collections in a form suitable for church use, like Chandler or Neale.

Others found that the public adopted their books against their intentions—for example Isaac Williams, who had written his translations in unusual metres on purpose to prevent their being sung. None of these was ever authorised, however.

In 1857 a number of clergymen, including Sir H. W. Baker, formed a committee to compile a hymn-book for the Church of England which should supersede all others. It was to be comprehensive, authoritative, and authorised. The proposal met with considerable support, and the upshot was the publication in 1860–1861 of *Hymns Ancient and Modern*, which has in fact held a dominant place ever since.

AMERICA. 1755–1875

The hymnody of Colonial America ran parallel to that of England. Watts and Wesley were as much drawn upon in the one as in the other, and compilations made in either country were interchangeable. Among the notable early hymn-writers of America is Samuel Davis, the fourth President of the College of New Jersey (now Princeton). But his few hymns are essentially the minor and supplementary work of one whose career was mostly that of a typical eighteenth-century virtuoso preacher.

But a genuinely native spirit is shown by the popularity of a hymn which was written, or at least first published, in London. This is *Christ the Appletree* (1761). It was naturalised by adoption in America, and with such other hymns as *Poor Wayfaring Stranger*, it represents a number which seem redolent, not only of religious spirit, but of the land itself. Most of them are anonymous. There is a vivid sense behind these hymns of the rich and boundless pastoral territory of what has been described as the "new green world". America was the Promised Land for unending miles west: and when these early hymns speak of Jordan, there seem to roll under the biblical name the actual waters of the Ohio, the Mississippi and the Missouri. To many of the minor sects of Europe America was a land of refuge where, if they sometimes found new persecutions, it was also possible to find a new freedom. Of these groups the Shakers are typical; they came to America in 1774 guided by their matriarchal leader, "Ann the Word", and established colonies which practised communism, celibacy and pacifism. In their songs too the abundant presence of nature is celebrated. And this is, as we shall see, a strain which has not faded away.

Hymns were written sporadically by the cultivated throughout the early part of the nineteenth century, but their way to general acceptance was an unsmooth one. A widespread prejudice against hymns existed in America until well into the second half of the century, which was eventually broken down by the writing of hymns by such well-known authors as Julia Ward Howe and Lydia Sigourney. A strange result of the Civil War was the discovery of a whole world of music in the Negro slave-songs and Spirituals, a beautiful form of folk-song which it is now believed was probably founded upon the camp-meeting songs discussed in the following section.

BRITISH AND AMERICAN REVIVAL. 1839–1953

A great flowering of hymnody took place in America and England during the nineteenth century in the cause of revival. Revival assumed several forms, from the purely religious manifestation to the temperance revival. Ever since Hogarth published his engravings of the squalor of "Gin Lane" contrasted with the prosperity of "Beer Street", reformers had been contesting the appalling influence of strong drink. The first temperance society was founded in New York in 1808; the first in Europe at Skibbereen in Ireland ten years later. The movement spread rapidly, its greatest success being the work of the Rev. Theobald Matthew of Cork, through whose preaching the consumption of liquor in Ireland dropped by half in 1838–42; the total of Irish who took the pledge exceeded the whole population of the country today. By the nineteenth century the claim of beer as a preferable alternative to spirits had been liquidated in favour of water, to which the drunkard was exhorted to turn in hymn, chorus and dramatic verse, in the name and with the help of God.

The strictly religious revival meeting dates from the great Kentucky Revival of 1800, to which wandering preachers of different denominations, working together, drew enormous gatherings up to 20,000 people all of whom sang, shouted and shook hands all round. Three thousand at a time would faint and have to be revived. At other times during the singing the strains of several hymns would all be competing for attention at once in various parts of the crowd, while the singers bellowed at the tops of their voices and jerked their limbs about. In 1805 Lorenzo Dow, a Methodist preacher, came to England, and began holding camp-meetings around the countryside. An outcome of this was the expulsion from the Methodist Church of his follower Hugh Bourne, who then proceeded to found the Primitive Methodist Church.

These meetings developed a hymnody of their own—or rather adapted already current hymns to their own uses by adding choruses and refrains sandwiched into the verses. Each chorus could be adapted to several hymns as necessary. Here, for example, is a couplet by Charles Wesley in its extended camp-meeting form:

> "He comes, He comes, the Judge severe,
>> Roll, Jordan, roll!
> The Seventh Trumpet speaks him near,
>> Roll, Jordan, roll!

Chorus

>> I want to go to Heaven, I do,
>>> Hallelujah, Lord!
>> We'll praise the Lord in heaven above,
>>> Roll, Jordan, roll!"

For an English example of this sort of revision we may take the version of H. F. Lyte's *The Pilgrim's Song* (see p. 200), used in a hymn-book compiled by Richard Weaver, the converted collier, in 1861. Such singers as Weaver interpolated a verse:

> "The winds of Affliction around me may blow,
> And dash my lone bark as I'm sailing below;
> I smile at the storm as I lean on his breast,
> And soon I shall land in the haven of rest."

They also added a chorus:

> "For the Lion of Judah shall break every chain,
> And give us the victory again and again."

These movements, however, produced no notable hymn-writers of their own to whom it is possible to attach a name, though some anonymous hymns have a wonderful rush and sweep of enthusiasm. Hymns were an indispensable part of the early revivals; but not a moving force in them.

The case was altered by the great missionary work of Dwight Moody and Ira D. Sankey from 1870 onwards. Sacred song was a mainspring of their activity, as they planned from the outset and exploited to the full. The hymn became a powerful instrument of conversion in their hands; the leaders of the movement spoke and wrote of their successes as "Song Victories". The very mention of their names was liable to touch off unforeseen bursts of vocal melody. At the height of their fame, one cross-talk comedian addressed to his partner the innocuous question, "Are you moody (Moody) today?" "No," came the reply, "but I feel Sankey-monious (sanctimonious)!"—whereupon, to the consternation of the jokers, the audience rose to their feet as one man and sang in unison, "Nearer, my God, to Thee". So widespread was the effect of Moody and Sankey's work that Baring-Gould remarked sourly in a preface to a collection of *Church Songs* (1884), "We have become a nation of hymn-singers".

Most of the musical work was carried out by Sankey, a fine singer, who was largely responsible for compiling the movement's song-books. He drew to a certain extent on the writers of the seventeenth and eighteenth centuries; but spent more energy gathering the works of contemporary authors, to such effect that the 1912 edition of his *Sacred Songs and Solos* contained nearly thirteen hundred pieces. In doing so he established the most recent marked style of evangelistic hymnody. It descends, with its lively choruses, from camp-meeting hymnody, while in its longing for Jerusalem, best expressed in Lowry's "Shall we gather at the river", it returns to the native pastoral feeling of early American hymns.

Horatius Bonar, already old and well-known, had written many hymns which Sankey adapted with his enthusiastic support. Fanny Crosby, R. S. Lowry, E. A. Hoffman and others were found in this way, and identified themselves closely with the work. Their hymns are still staple material for camp-meetings, and in America have almost passed into the realm of folk-song. Many of them in Sankey's lifetime accumulated their own legends; indeed there often seemed something inspired about his discovery of them. Elizabeth Clephane's "The ninety and nine", written on the death of her brother, a remittance man, was discovered by Sankey over twenty years later in a newspaper casually picked up in a railway carriage. It became one of the most effective hymns of the revival movement, and many stories are told of its prowess. On one occasion Sankey sang it on the steps of an old Connecticut church. The air was clear, the building acted as a sounding board and his voice carried half a mile across the river to a man who had refused to attend the meeting. It was not long before that man, too, was converted.

Fanny Crosby, the "Sightless Songstress", was perhaps the most voluble of Sankey's recruits to hymnody; between 1863 and 1915, the year of her death, she is credited with an output of 8,000 hymns; a productivity which became a source of embarrassment to her publishers, who were forced to issue them under a hundred pseudonyms. The greatest of Sankey's colleagues was, however, P. P. Bliss, although his death in the

Ashtabula train disaster cut short their association after only two years. He associated himself so closely with the work that he used to subscribe letters "Gospelsongfully yours". Most of his hymns were occasional, written to stories Moody told during his addresses; and they were immensely effective. "I should think," wrote Sankey, "Mr. Bliss's 'Almost persuaded' has won more souls to the Saviour than any other song written by him." But the songs went a good deal further than England or America; a missionary of the time entered a Zulu kraal to rest, and heard the unexpected strains of "Hold the Fort" on the lips of its owner.

The Southern States of America are today the most productive area in the world for hymns. Perhaps nowhere else has hymn-writing been so markedly a stepping-stone for a career. The numerous hymn-singing groups that are active provide writers with an eager audience. As their work becomes more popular, they find it is published more frequently; eventually they become anthologists and compilers, finally small publishers turning out large numbers of hymn-books yearly, themselves employing other new writers. The output claimed by some of these writers far surpasses that of even such dedicated authors as Charles Wesley and Fanny Crosby.

Just like such popular poems as ballads and limericks, hymns have been subject to alteration at whatever hands have seen fit to remould them; and in some, changes have taken place not at one blow, but in many stages. This may be illustrated from one of the best-known and most favourite of hymns. The verse by Charles Wesley:

> "Jesu, Lover of my soul,
>   Let me to Thy bosom fly,
>   While the nearer waters roll,
>   While the tempest still is nigh",

has been twisted a dozen ways since he published it in 1740. The opening phrase has become "Jesu, Refuge of my soul",

2   33

"Jesus, Saviour of my soul", "Father, Refuge of my soul". At different times the second line has read, "To Thy sheltering arms we fly" (1815); "To Thy sheltering cross we fly" (1819); "Let me to Thy mercy fly" (1821). The third line has suffered many sea-changes, among which are: "While the billows near me roll" (1764); "While the raging billows roll" (1788); "While the threat'ning waters roll" (1810).

A great deal of such re-writing was undertaken by the editors of *Hymns Ancient and Modern*, whose high standards led them to re-write what they considered unpromising originals into lines which are now among the most familiar in hymnody. John Chandler's opening line to his translation of the *Victis Sibi Cognomina*, for instance, runs:

"'Tis for conquering kings to gain".

After revision for *Hymns Ancient and Modern* it emerged almost unrecognisable but destined for fame as:

"Conquering kings their titles take
From the foes they captive make".

Such alterations have not always—indeed, not usually—been made for the sake of euphony or style. Once written, a good hymn has in the past usually become, for all practical purposes, common property. It has accordingly been adopted by all and sundry, whether they shared the tenets of its original author or not. As ancient Egyptian kings adopted the historical inscriptions of their predecessors by the simple process of substituting their own names for the original builders', alterations have often been executed to bring the hymn into congruity with the beliefs with which it must now accord; and they have been made without hesitation or acknowledgement. The reasons have of course been other than doctrinal in many cases. They have been intended to smooth awkward lines, to adapt them more comfortably to the singing throats of the congregation. There is no doubt that some have also been intended to spare the sensibilities of the congregation: for instance the line in

Toplady's *Rock of Ages* which is now generally seen as "When my eyelids close in death", was written as the hair-raising image, "When my eye-strings break in death". As so many times before and since, the editors have turned boldness and poetry into acceptable but flat verse. The consequence is that many congregations sing versions of hymns far removed from those their authors intended without any idea that they are doing so.

There is no doubt, however, that the authors, or many of them, would have strong feelings on the matter. Indeed, Geoffrey Thring, in the preface of his collection of hymns, writes that he is perfectly prepared for them to be used without acknowledgement and has nothing against this so long as they are used accurately.

To restore the hymns included in this book to the versions the authors wrote has been not merely a work of piety, but an indication of a belief that they knew best; and even when they did not—for not all the revisions have been for the worse—that their own words have a peculiar interest. In every case they stand, more exactly than anyone else's words can, for the author's beliefs. His punctuation alone can tell us of his state of mind: dashes and exclamation marks can be indications of an enthusiasm typical of himself and his period. Sacred names and pronouns were capitalised at different times according to different usages, some of which appear very odd to eyes accustomed to the nineteenth-century practice of capitalising everywhere it is conceivably possible. In the true versions of these hymns it is possible to see reflected something of the history of the church.

Accordingly, we have used the earliest texts available: few of those given here are not derived from the first printings of these hymns, although some are taken from the authors' own latest revisions. As and when the inevitable problems involved with the editing of any text written before 1900 have arisen, we have done our best to avoid pedantry but achieve accuracy. No corrections have been made in spelling or punctuation, though a few misprints which would clearly have been recognised as such by contemporaries have been silently corrected. So have a few qualifications such as "Another Hymn" when its preceding one is not included, and the common practice of numbering the verses has nowhere been retained.

Everyone who has used a hymn-book which has the tunes printed in it is familiar with the stave filled with fat breves, the *mf, pp, dim,* and the way that the tunes are classified by the number of lines and number of feet in the verse they are to accompany. Revivalists have more straightforward direction, "Trustingly and hopefully", or "Slowly with emotion". But though the purpose of this book is to isolate the hymns from music, a word must be said about the tunes.

At the Reformation the Prayer Books of 1549 and 1552, in their effort to simplify the services, left no directions about the music to be used at the services. Wither was the first person to attempt a hymn-book with his *Hymns and Songs of the Church,* which had sixteen tunes by Orlando Gibbons; though Tallis contributed to John Daye's *Morning and Evening Prayer and Communion* in 1565, these were not tunes specifically written for hymns, although they have been used for them since. The Scotch Psalter of 1635 had 143 tunes taken from British and Continental sources, but during the seventeenth century the number of tunes in use for the psalms declined. Lining-out was no encouragement to musicians. Up to the middle of the eighteenth century hymns were sung to psalm tunes; Watts had psalm tunes in mind when he wrote his hymns; later in the century when the number of good hymns was greatly increased by the work of Watts and Wesley, the new tunes which were written for them kept the solidity of the old psalm tunes. At the time that English music became influenced by Handel there was a movement to popularise music similar to the German chorales. Later the Methodists, like the revivalists of this century, adapted secular tunes to sacred songs. At the beginning of the last century more music began to be written specifically for hymns, and with the Oxford Movement there was a great increase in the number of hymn tunes written; many of them were based on ancient models, some on the often inferior music used by the Church of Rome at the time. Now, even if there is a decline in the number of good hymns, the musicians have caught up and lively hymn tunes are being written, a change from the belief that slowness and tedium make a tune holy.

HYMNS AS POETRY

ROMAN CATHOLIC
and
CHURCH OF ENGLAND
1560–1655

William Kethe. ? –1608

PSALME C

Al people y^t on earth do dwel,
    sing to ye lord, with chereful voice
Him serve w^t fear, his praise forth tel,
    come ye before him and reioyce.

The Lord ye know is God in dede,
    with out our aide, he did us make:
We are his folck, he doth us fede,
    and for his Shepe, he doth us take.

Oh enter then his gates with prayse
    approche with ioye, his courtes unto:
Praise, laude, and blesse his name alwayes,
    for it is semely so to doe.

For why? the Lord our God is good,
    his mercy is for euer sure:
His trueth at all tymes firmely stood
    and shall from age to age indure.

J. Daye's Psalter, 1560–1.

F. B. P.

A SONG MAD BY F. B. P.

(To the tune of Diana)

Hierusalem my happie home
　　When shall I come to thee
When shall my sorrowes haue an end
　　Thy ioyes when shall I see

O happie harbour of the saints
　　O sweete and pleasant soyle
In thee noe sorrow may be founde
　　No greefe, noe care, noe toyle

In thee noe sickenesse may be seene
　　Noe hurt, no ache, noe sore
There is noe death, nor uglie devill
　　There is life for euermore

Noe dampishe mist is seene in thee
　　Noe could, nor darksome night
There everie soule shines as the sunn
　　There god himselfe giues light

There lust and lukar cannot dwell
　　There envie beares no sway
There is no hunger heate nor coulde
　　But pleasure everie way

Hierusalem: Hierusalem
　　God grant I once may see
Thy endless ioyes and of the same
　　Partaker aye to bee

42

Thy wales are made of precious stones
    Thy bulwarkes Diamondes square
Thy gates are of right orient pearle
    Exceedinge riche and rare

Thy terrettes and thy pinacles
    With carbuncles doe shine
Thy verie streetes are paued with gould
    Surpassinge cleare and fine

Thy houses are of Ivorie
    Thy windoes cristale cleare
Thy tyles are mad of beaten gould
    O god that I were there

Within thy gates nothinge doeth come
    That is not passinge cleane
Noe spiders web, noe durt noe dust
    Noe filthe may there be seene

Ah my sweete home Hierusalem
    Would god I were in thee
Would god my woes were at an end
    Thy ioyes that I might see

Thy saints are crownd with glorie great
    They see god face to face
They triumph still, they still reioyce
    Most happie is their case

Wee that are here in banishment
    Continuallie doe mourne
We sighe and sobbe, we weepe and weale
    Perpetually we groane

Our sweete is mixt with bitter gaule
    Our pleasure is but paine
Our ioyes scarce last the lookeing on
    Our sorrowes still remaine

But there they liue in such delight
    Such pleasure and such play
As that to them a thousand yeares
    Doth seeme as yeaster day

Thy viniardes and thy orchardes are
    Most beutifull and faire
Full furnished with trees and fruits
    Most wonderfull and rare

Thy gardens and thy gallant walkes
    Continually are greene
There groes such sweete and pleasant flowers
    As noe where eles are seene

There is nector and ambrosia made
    There is muske and civette sweete
There manie a faire and daintie drugge
    Are troden under feete

There cinomon there sugar groes
    There narde and balme abound
What tounge can tell or hart conceiue
    The ioyes that there are found

Quyt through the streetes with siluer sound
    The flood of life doe flowe
Upon whose bankes on everie syde
    The wood of life doth growe

There trees for euermore beare fruite
    And euermore doe springe
There euermore the Angels sit
    And euermore doe singe

There David standes with harpe in hand
    As maister of the Queere
Tenne thousand times that man were blest
    That might this musicke hear

Our Ladie singes magnificat
  With tune surpassinge sweete
And all the virginns beare their parts
  Sitinge aboue her feete

Te Deum doth Sant Ambrose singe
  Saint Augustine dothe the like
Ould Simeon and Zacharie
  Haue not their songes to seeke

There Magdalene hath left her mone
  And cheerefullie doth singe
With blessed Saints whose harmonie
  In everie streete doth ringe

Hierusalem my happie home
  Would god I were in thee
Would god my woes were at an end
  Thy ioyes that I might see

finis   finis

British Museum Additional Manuscripts 15,225

Thomas Campion. ?–1619

Come let us sound with melody the praises
Of the kings king, Th'omnipotent creator,
Author of number, that hath all the world
              In harmonie framed.

Heav'n is his throne perpetually shining,
His devine power and glorie thence he thunders
One in all, and all still in one abiding,
              Both Father and Sonne.

O sacred sprite invisible, eternall,
Ev'ry where, yet unlimited, that all things
Canst in one moment penetrate, revive me
　　　　O holy Spirit.

Rescue, O rescue me from earthly darknes,
Banish hence all these elementall objects,
Guide my soule, that thirsts, to the lively Fountaine
　　　　Of thy devinenes.

Cleanse my soul, O God, thy bespotted Image
Altered with sinne, so that heav'nly purenes
Cannot acknowledge me but in thy mercies
　　　　O Father of grace.

But when once thy beames do remove my darknes,
O then I'le shine forth as an Angell of light,
And record with more than an earthly voice thy
　　　　Infinite honours.

A Booke of Ayres, 1601

Never weather-beaten saile more willing bent to shore,
Never tyred Pilgrims limbes affected slumber more;
Then my weary spright now longs to flye out of my troubled
　　brest.
　　O come quickly sweetest Lord, and take my soule to rest.

Ever-blooming are the ioyes of Heav'ns high paradice,
Cold age deafes not there our eares, nor vapour dim our eyes;
Glory there the Sun out-shines, whose beames the blessed
　　　　onely see:
　　Come quickly glorious Lord, and raise my spright to thee.

Two Bookes of Ayres, 1613

John Donne. 1572–1631

A HYMNE TO GOD THE FATHER

Wilt thou forgive that sinne where I begunne,
　　Which was my sin, though it were done before?
Wilt thou forgive that sinne; through which I runne,
　　And do run still: though still I do deplore?
　　　　When thou has done, thou hast not done,
　　　　　For, I have more.

Wilt thou forgive that sinne which I have wonne
　　Others to sinne? and, made my sinne their doore?
Wilt thou forgive that sinne which I did shunne
　　A yeare, or two: but wallowed in, a score?
　　　　When thou has done, thou hast not done,
　　　　　For I have more.

I have a sinne of feare, that when I have spunne
　　My last thred, I shall perish on the shore;
But sweare by thy selfe, that at my death thy sonne
　　Shall shine as he shines now, and heretofore;
　　　　And, having done that, Thou haste done,
　　　　　I fear no more.

Poems, 1633

Phineas Fletcher. 1582–1650

AN HYMNE

Drop, drop, slow tears,
　　and bathe those beauteous feet,
Which brought from heav'n
　　the news and Prince of peace:
Cease not, wet eyes,
　　his mercies to intreat;

To crie for vengeance
    sinne doth never cease:
In your deep flouds
    drown all my faults and fears;
Nor let his eye
    see sinne, but through my tears.

The Purple Island, 1633

George Herbert. 1593–1633

ANTIPHON

Cho. Let all the world in ev'ry corner sing
    My God and King.

Vers. The heav'ns are not too high,
    His praise may thither flie:
    The earth is not too low,
    His praises there may grow.

Cho. Let all the world in ev'ry corner sing,
    My God and King.

Vers. The church with psalms must shout
    No doore can keep them out:
    But above all, the heart
    Must bear the longest part.

Cho. Let all the world in ev'ry corner sing,
    My God and King.

L'ENVOY

King of glorie, King of peace,
With the one make warre to cease;
With the other blesse thy sheep,
Thee to love, in thee to sleep.

Let not Sinne devoure thy fold,
Bragging that thy bloud is cold,
That thy death is also dead,
While his conquests dayly spread;
That thy flesh hath lost his food,
And thy Crosse is common wood.
Choke him, let him say no more,
But reserve his breath in store,
Till thy conquests and his fall
Make his sighs to use it all,
And then bargain with the winde
To discharge what is behinde.

The Temple, 1633

Sir Thomas Browne. 1605–1682

The night is come like to the day,
Depart not thou great God away.
Let not my sinnes, blacke as the night,
Eclipse the lustre of thy light.
Keepe still in my Horizon, for to me,
The Sunne makes not the day, but thee.
Thou whose nature cannot sleepe,
On my temples centry keepe;
Guard me 'gainst those watchfull foes,
Whose eyes are open while mine close.
Let no dreames my head infest,
But such as *Jacobs* temples blest.
While I doe rest, my soule advance,
Make my sleepe a holy trance:
That I may, my rest being wrought,
Awake into some holy thought.
And with as active vigour runne
My course, as doth the nimble Sunne.
Sleepe is a death, O make me try,
By sleeping, what it is to die.

And as gently lay my head
On my Grave, as now my bed.
How ere I rest, great God, let me
Awake againe at last with thee.
And thus assur'd, behold I lie
Securely, or to wake or die.
These are my drowsie dayes, in vaine
I doe now wake to sleepe againe.
O come that houre, when I shall never
Sleepe againe, but wake for ever!

Religio Medici, 1643

John Hall. 1627–1656

A PASTOROLL HYMNE

Happy Choristers of Aire,
Who by your nimble flight draw neare
    His throne, whose wondrous story
    And unconfined glory
Your notes still Caroll, whom your sound
And whom your plumy pipes rebound.

Yet do the lazy Snailes no lesse
The greatnesse of our Lord confesse,
    And those whom weight hath chain'd
    And to the Earth restrain'd,
Their ruder voices do as well,
Yea and the speechlesse Fishes tell.

Great Lord, from whom each Tree receaves,
Then paies againe as rent, his leaves;
    Thou dost in purple set,
    The Rose and Violet,
And giv'st the sickly Lilly white,
Yet in them all, thy name dost write.

Divine Poems, 1647

Henry Vaughan. 1622–1695

ASCENSION-HYMN

They are all gone into the world of light!
    And I alone sit lingring here;
Their very memory is fair and bright,
    And my sad thoughts doth clear.

It glows and glitters in my cloudy brest
    Like stars upon some gloomy grove,
Or those faint beams in which this hill is drest,
    After the Sun's remove.

I see them walking in an Air of glory,
    Whose light doth trample on my days:
My days, which are at best but dull and hoary,
    Meer glimering and decays.

O holy hope! and high humility,
    High as the Heavens above!
These are your walks, and you have shew'd them me
    To kindle my cold love,

Dear, beauteous death! the Jewel of the Just,
    Shining no where, but in the dark;
What mysteries do lie beyond thy dust;
    Could man outlook that mark!

He that hath found some fledg'd birds nest, may know
    At first sight, if the bird be flown;
But what fair Well, or Grove he sings in now,
    That is to him unknown.

And yet, as Angels in some brighter dreams
    Call to the soul, when man doth sleep:
So some strange thoughts transcend our wonted theams,
    And into glory peep.

If a star were confin'd into a Tomb
    Her captive flames must needs burn there;
But when the hand that lockt her up, gives room,
    She'l shine through all the sphaere.

O Father of eternal life, and all
    Created glories under thee!
Resume thy spirit from this world of thrall
    Into true liberty.

Either disperse these mists, which blot and fill
    My perspective (still) as they pass,
Or else remove me hence unto that hill,
    Where I shall need no glass.

Silex Scintillans, 1655

SCOTLAND AND DISSENTERS
1578–1697

James Wedderburn. 1495 ?–1553
John Wedderburn. 1500 ?–1556
Robert Wedderburn. 1510 ?–1557 ?

Quho is at my windo? quho, quho?
Go from my windo, go, go!
Quho callis thair, sa lyke a strangair?
    Go from my windo, go!

Lord, I am heir, ane wretchit mortall,
That for thy mercy dois cry and call
Unto thé, my Lord celestiall.
    Se quho is at my windo, quho.

How dar thow for mercy cry,
Sa lang in sin as thow dois ly?
Mercy to haue thow art not worthy.
    Go from my windo, go.

My gylt, gude Lord, I will refuse,
And the wickit lyfe that I did use,
Traistand thy mercy sall be myne excuse.
    Se quho is at my windo, quho.

To be excusit, thow wald richt faine,
In spending of thy lyfe in vaine,
Hauing my Gospell in greit disdaine.
    Go from my windo, go.

O Lord, I haue offendit thé,
Excuse thairof thair can nane be:
I haue followit them that sa teichit me.
    Se quho is at my windo, quho.

Nay, I call thé nocht fra my dure, I wis,
Lyke any stranger that unknawin is;
Thow art my brother, and my will it is,
    That in at my dure thow go.

With richt humbill hart, Lord, thé I pray,
Thy comfort and grace obteine I may:
Schaw me the paith and reddy way
    In at thy dure for to go.

I am cheif gyde to riche and pure,
Schawand the paithway richt to my dure,
I am thair comfort in euerie hour,
    That in at my dure will go.

Bot thay that walk ane other way,
As mony did teiche from day to day,
Thay wer indurit, my Gospell did say,
    And far from my dure sall go.

O gracious Lord, comfort of all wicht,
For thy greit power, and cheif excellent micht,
Sen thow art gyde, and verray licht,
    In at thy dure let me go.

Man, I gaue thé nocht fre will
That thow suld my Gospell spill;
Thow dois na gude bot euer ill;
    Thairfoir from my dure that thow go.

That will, allace, hes my begylit,
That will sa sair hes me defylit,
That will thy presence hes me exilit;
    Zit at thy dure lat me go.

To blame that will, thow dois not richt,
I gaue thé ressoun, quhairby thow micht
Haue knawin the day by the dark nicht,
    In at my dure for to go.

Lord, I pray thé with all my hart,
Of thy greit mercy remufe my smart,
Lat ane drop of thy grace be my part,
    That in at thy dure I may go.

I haue spokin in my Scripture,
I will the deid of na creature;
Quha will ask mercy, sall be sure
    And in at my dure for to go.

O Lord, quhais mercy is but end,
Quhairin ocht to thé I did offend,
Grant me space my lyfe to amend,
    That in at thy dure I may go.

Remember thy sin, and als thy smart,
And als for thé quhat was my part:
Remember the speir that thirlit my hart,
    And in at my dure thow sall go.

And it wer zit till do againe,
Rather or thow suld ly in paine,
I wald suffer mair in certaine,
    That in at my dure thow micht go.

I ask na thing of thé thairfoir,
Bot lufe for lufe, to lay in stoir;
Gif me thy hart, I ask no moir,
    And in at my dure thow sall go.

O gracious Lord celestiall,
As thow art Lord and King eternall,
Grant us grace, that we may enter all,
    And in at thy dure for to go.

Quho is at my windo? quho?
Go from my windo, go!
Cry na mair thair, lyke ane stranger,
  Bot in at my dure thow go.

*   *   *

With huntis up, with huntis up,
  It is now perfite day,
Jesus, our King, is gane in hunting,
  Quha lykis to speid thay may.

Ane cursit fox lay hid in rox
  This lang and mony ane day,
Deuouring scheip, quhill he micht creip,
  Nane micht him schaip away.

It did him gude to laip the blude
  Of zoung and tender lammis;
Nane culd he mis, for all was his,
  The zoung anis with thair dammis.

The hunter is Christ, that huntis in haist,
  The hundis ar Peter and Paull,
The Paip is the foxe, Rome is the rox,
  That rubbis us on the gall.

That cruell beist, he neuer ceist,
  Be his usurpit power,
Under dispens to get our penneis,
  Our saulis to deuoir.

Quha culd deuyse sic merchandise
  As he had thair to sell,
Onles it war proud Lucifer,
  The greit maister of Hell.

56

He had to sell the Tantonie bell,
    And pardonis thairin was;
Remissioun of sinnis in auld scheip skinnis,
    Our saulis to bring from grace.

With bullis of leid, quhyte wax and reid,
    And uther quhylis with grene,
Closit in ane box, this usit the fox,
    Sic peltrie was neuer sene.

With dispensatiounis and obligatiounis,
    According to his law,
He wald dispens, for money from hence,
    With thame he neuer saw.

To curs and ban the sempill pure man,
    That had nocht to flé the paine;
Bot quhen he had payit all to ane myte,
    He mon be obsoluit than.

To sum, God wot, he gaue tot quot,
    And uther sum pluralitie;
Bot first with penneis he mon dispens,
    Or ellis it will nocht be.

Kingis to marie, and sum to tarie,
    Sic is his power and micht,
Quha that hes gold, with him will he hold,
    Thocht it be contrair all richt.

O blissit Peter, the foxe, is ane lier,
    Thow knawis weill it is nocht sa,
Quhill at the last, he salbe downe cast
    His peltrie, pardonis, and all.

The Gude and Godlie Ballates, 1578

George Wither. 1588–1667

A GENERALL INVITATION TO PRAISE GOD

This Hymn *stirreth up to the praise of God, by a Poeticall Invitation of the* Creatures *to the performance of that Dutie according to their severall Faculties and Dignities. And, it is a preamble to the following* Hymns.

Come, oh come in pious *Laies,*
Sound we *God-Almighti's* praise.
Hither bring in one Consent,
Heart, and Voice, and Instrument.
Musick adde of ev'ry kinde;
Sound the Trump, the Cornet winde.
Strike the Violl, touch the Lute.
Let nor Tongue, nor String be mute:
    Nor a Creature dumb be found,
    That hath either Voice or Sound.

Let those Things which do not live
In *Still-Musick,* praises give.
Lowly pipe, ye *Wormes* that creep,
On the *Earth,* or in the *Deep.*
Loud-aloft, your Voices strain,
Beasts, and *Monsters* of the Main.
Birds, your warbling *Treble* sing.
Clouds, your *Peales of Thunders* ring.
    Sun and *Moon,* exalted higher,
    And bright *Stars,* augment this *Quire.*

Come ye *Sons* of *Humane-Race,*
In this *Chorus* take a place;
And, amid the mortall-Throng,
Be you *Masters of the Song.*
Angels, and supernall Pow'rs,
Be the noblest *Tenor* yours.

Let in praise of *God*, the sound
Run a *never-ending Round*;
 That our *Song of praise* may be
 Everlasting as is *HE*.

From *Earths* vast and hollow wombe,
Musicks deepest *Base* may come.
Seas and *Flouds*, from shore to shoare,
Shall their *Counter Tenors* roare.
To this *Consort*, (when we sing)
Whistling *Winds*, your *Descants* bring.
That our *Song* may over clime,
All the Bounds of *Place* and *Time*,
 And ascend from *Sphere* to *Sphere*,
 To the great *All-mightie's* eare.

So, from Heaven, on Earth, he shall
Let his gracious Blessings fall;
And this huge wide *Orbe*, we see
Shall one *Quire*, one *Temple* be;
Where, in such a *Praise*, full Tone
We will sing, what he hath done,
That the cursed *Fiends* below,
Shall thereat impatient grow.
 Then, oh Come, in pious *Laies*,
 Sound we *God-Almighties* praise.

WHEN WE RIDE FOR PLEASURE

We make use of GOD'S *Creatures, as well for pleasure, as for necessity. Therefore when we ride forth for pleasure, it will become us to mix, now and then such thankfull Meditations with our lawfull Pleasure, as are in this* Hymne.

(Sing this as the 10 Commandments)

My GOD, how kind? how good are thou?
Of Man, how great is thy regard?

Who do'st all needfull things allow,
And, some for Pleasure, hast prepar'd?
    With what great Speed? with how much ease?
On this thy Creature, am I borne,
Which at my will, and when I please
Doth forward goe, and backe returne?

Why should not I, ô gracious GOD!
More plyant be to thy command,
When I am guided by thy word,
And gently reined by thy hand.
    Asham'd I may become to see
The *Beast* (which knowes nor good, nor ill)
More faithfull in obeying me,
Then I have been, to do thy will.

From him therefore, LORD, let me learn
To serve thee, better then I do;
And minde how much it may concern
My welfare to endeavour so.
    And though I know, this Creature lent
As well for Pleasure, as for need;
That I the wrong thereof prevent,
Let me, still, carefully take heed.

For, he that, wilfully shall dare
That Creature, to oppress or grieve,
Which GOD to serve him doth prepare,
Himself of Mercy doth deprive.
    And *He*, or *His* (unlesse in time
They doe repent of that abuse)
Shall one day suffer for his Crime;
And want such *Creatures*, for their use.

FOR ONE UPBRAIDED WITH DEFORMITIE

To some this is a very great Affliction, and they who are sensible of other mens Passions, will not thinke it impertinently added; if this Hymn be inserted, to comfort such as are upbraided, or afflicted through their bodily defects, in this kind; and to instruct their Despisers.

(Sing this, as the Magnificat)

LORD, though I murmur not, at thee,
 For that in other Eies,
I, so deformed, seem to be,
 That, me, they do despise:
Yet, their contempt, and their disdain
 My heart afflicteth so,
That for mine ease, I now complain,
 My secret grief, to show.

Thou knows't, oh GOD! it was not I,
 Who did this Bodie frame,
On which they cast a scornefull eie;
 By whom I flouted am
Thou knows't likewise it was not *they*,
 Who did their Bodies make;
Although on my defects to play,
 Occasions, oft they take.

Then, why should they have Love, or Fame,
 For what they have not done?
Or, why should I have scorn or shame,
 For what I could not shun?
Thy workmanship, I am, oh LORD,
 Though they do me deride:
And, thou, by what they have abhorr'd,
 Are, some way, glorifide.

Therefore, since thou this way hast chose,
 To humble me on Earth.

My imperfections now dispose,
    To help my *second Birth*.
Let me in Thee contentment find:
    And, lovely make thou me,
By those perfections of the *Mind*,
    Which dearest are to Thee.

Since, *Features* none, in me appear,
    To win a *fleshly Love*;
Let those, which priz'd by others are,
    My passions never move.
But, quench thou, all those youthfull Fires,
    Which in my brest do burn;
And, all my Lusts, and vain Desires,
    To sacred *motions* turn.

So, though in secret grief, I spend
    The Life that nature gave;
I, shall have comforts, in the end,
    And, gain a blessed Grave;
From whence, the *Flesh* which now I wear,
    In glory, shall arise;
And, fully beautifide appear,
    In all beholders eyes.

Haleluiah, or, Britans Second Remembrancer. 1641

William Barton. 1598?–1678

HYMN, CELEBRATES NAZEBY, AND OTHER GREAT VICTORIES OF THE CHURCH

Judges 5, 2, 3.

Sing praises $\left\{\begin{array}{l}\text{Israel}\\\text{England}\end{array}\right\}$ to the Lord,
    that hath avenged thee;
When as the people went to fight,
    offring themselves so free.

Ye Kings give ear, ye Princes hear,
    I, even I will sing,
And sweetly raise my voyce in praise,
    To $\begin{Bmatrix} \text{Israels} \\ \text{Englands} \end{Bmatrix}$ God and King.

My heart is tow'rd the Governors   vers. 9, 10.
    that did their help afford,
Offering themselves so willingly,
    wherefore bless ye the Lord.
Ye Travellers and Passengers,
    and ye that ride in state,
And ye that yet in judgement sit,
    now speak it in the gate.

All they that are delivered,   vers. 11, 7.
    from $\begin{Bmatrix} \text{Archers} \\ \text{Gunners} \\ \text{Cannons} \end{Bmatrix}$ frightful noise,
The righteous acts of God the Lord,
    they shall rehearse with joys.
The Passengers were wanderers,
    in by-paths up and down,
And none $\begin{Bmatrix} \text{durst dwell in Israel} \\ \text{could dwel in England wel} \end{Bmatrix}$
    but in a walled Town.

Awake awake, O $\begin{Bmatrix} \text{Parliament,} \\ \text{Deborah,} \end{Bmatrix}$ vers. 12, 31.
    rise $\begin{Bmatrix} \text{Barak} \\ \text{Conqu'rors} \\ \text{Fairfax} \\ \text{Cromwel} \end{Bmatrix}$ sing a Song.
Lead captive $\begin{Bmatrix} \text{thy} \\ \text{your} \end{Bmatrix}$ captivity,
    come lead them all along:

So perish those that are thy foes;
 but Lord let all thy lovers
Be like the Sun when days begun,
 and brightest beams discovers.

Hallelujah, Or Certain Hymns Composed out of Scripture, to celebrate some Special and Publick Occasions, 1651

Benjamin Keach. 1640–1704

THE ROSE OF SHARON

Sharon the *Garden of the World*,
 the *Pride* of *Palestine*;
Whose *Natural soyl* more *Glory bore*
 than *Solomon could* resign;
Could ne'er produce so *sweet* a *Rose*
 as *I* will be to *Thee*.
So fair a *Lilly* never grew,
 Sharon must stoop to *Me*.

O Blessed Jesus, dost thou say,
 who'll have a Rose so sweet!
Who will refuse our *Sharons Rose,*
 that knows its *fragrant scent*?
Upon the Cross thou was *Distill'd,*
 we taste in *Distillation,*
The *sweetness* of the *absent Rose,*
 by *Faith* and *Acceptation.*

Thou art a *Rose*, my Soul's *repose,*
 O let me never be,
My *Dearest Lord*, a *Thorn* to thee,
 who art so *sweet* to me.
Thou art the *Lilly* of the *Vale,*
 a *matchless Purity.*
And I will sing thy Praise since thou
 dost in my *Bosom* ly.

64

A HYMN OF CHRIST'S DIVINE LOVE
On Cant. 1

Come near, come nearer yet and *move* thy sweetest Lips to *mine?*
For why, thy *Love*, who art all *Love*, excels the *choicest Wine!*
Like to an *Ointment Poured out*, is thy sweet *Name*, and *Favour;*
Wise Virgins compass thee about, for thy good *Ointments Savour.*

O *Draw me* with thy *Cords of Love!* we will run *after thee;*
The King into his *Chambers* hath in *Love* Conducted *me.*
Thy *rays* will make our *faces Shine*, in *thee* we will *rejoyce;*
Thy Love is *better* far than *Wine;* thou art the *upright's Choice!*

But O *thou, whom my Soul doth Love! Tell me,* O tell me soon,
Where *feeds* thy *Flock;* where *is the place* thou mak'st them rest at
    Noon?
Why should I *stray* and lose my *way?* till I at last do *fall*
Among thy *fellows Flocks* (as they themselves do proudly *Call*).

O *fairest One;* if thou wouldst know where thou shouldst *feed*
    and *ly,*
The *footsteps* of the *Flock will show* the *way* asuredly?

HIS EYES ARE LIKE THE EYES OF DOVES
Cant. v. 12

> *I'll tell you farther, that if such*
>   *A* Person *you shall see,*
> *Whose* Eyes *like* Doves *are wash't with* Milk
>   *and* Water *this is* he?
> *He hath* a killing Eye, *'twill* Pierce
>   *through* Adamantine *Ears;*
> *And* wound *a* Rock *but with a* look,
>   *and* melt *it into* Tears.

3

Eyes *that are* clear *and* fitly *set,*
　that can see all things past,
And *all things* present *and to* come,
　as long as Time *shall* last:
Whose Eyes are Pure, Holy and Chast,
　never defil'd *with* Sin;
That never was in the least Promp't
　to take foul Objects in.

If such a One *you* meet, *whose* Eyes
　like Flames, *and* Lamps *of* Fire
Strikes Dead, *and yet gives* Life *thereby,*
　tis he *that* I desire?
This is the Man *I* seek, *and* praise,
　All-seeing, *and* All-Eye:
Tell him, *if such a* one *you* meet,
　'*tis for* his Love, *I* Die!

A Feast of Fat Things, 1696

Joseph Stennett. 1663–1713

HYMN

Ps 84. 1, 2.	How sweet, how beauteous is the Place,
	Where God his Presence grants;
Ps. 128. 3.	His pious Children sitting round
	His Tabl' as Olive-Plants!
Cant. 5. 1.	To them he cries, My welcome Friends,
	Eat of this Feast of mine;
Prov. 9. 5.	Come, my Beloved, freely drink
	Of this my mingled Wine.
	LORD, we accept thy bounteous Treat
	With Wonder, Joy and Love:
Psal. 27. 4.	O may we in thy House have place,
	And ne're from thence remove.

Here let our Faith still feed on Thee,
    The only Food Divine;   John. 6.
To Faith thy Flesh is Meat indeed,   50. &c.
    The Blood the Noblest Wine:

Thy Blood, that purifying Juice,   1 Joh. 1. 7.
    To cleanse the Soul design'd;
To heal a Sinner's bleeding Heart,   Luk. 10. 34.
    And chear his drooping Mind.

Here we rejoice to see thy Love   1 Cor. 13. 12.
    Through Figures, and in part;
But how much greater Joy wil't be
    To see thee as thou art!   1 Joh. 3. 2.

HYMN

(As the 100 Psalm)

Wherewith shall I a sinful Worm   Mic. 6. 6.
Jehovah's Sanctu'ry draw nigh?
With what Oblations shall I bow
Before the Throne of God most High?

Shall I Burnt-Offerings to him bring,
Calves taken from their tender Dams?   Ver. 7.
Will God be pleas'd, if I should slay
A thousand and a thousand Rams?

Shall I upon his Altar pour
Rivers of Oil ten thousand times,
Or my First-born an Offering make,
To expiate my odious Crimes?

No —— God is so incens'd by Sin,   Psal. 40. 6.
Such Offerings all would be in vain,   Ps. 51. 16.
Too mean to save the guilty Soul,
And purge it from so foul a Stain.

Heb. 6. 18.	With broken Heart and Fervent Cries,
	Dear JESUS, to thy Cross I fly;
Heb. 7. 25.	Tho other Refuge fail, on Thee
	My Soul with Safety can rely.

Luk. 10. 34.	The Blood that issu'd from thy Wounds,
	Becomes both Oil and Wine to ours;
Job. 34. 29.	No Ease, until thy Hand this Balm
	Into the wounded Conscience pours.

As at thy Table we behold
Thy All-sufficient Sacrifice,

Isa. 53. 5.	Let's feel the Virtue of thy Blood,
Joh. 6. 54.	Which heals, and chears, and purifies.
1. Joh. 1. 7.	

Psal. 43. 4.	So while our Feet stand in thy Courts,
Ps. 116. 17.	To Thee, O God, our Life and Joy,
Ps. 103. 1.	We'll bring the Sacrifice of Praise,
	In Praise our Hearts and Tongues employ.

Hymns in Commemoration of the Sufferings of our Blessed Saviour Jesus Christ, 1697

CHURCH OF ENGLAND
1683–1712

John Mason. 1646–1694

A SONG OF PRAISE FOR THE LORDS DAY

Blest day of God, most Calm, most bright;
    The first and best of days.
The Lab'rours Rest, the Saints delight,
    A day of Mirth and praise.
My Saviours Face did make thee Shine.
    His Rising did thee Raise.
This made thee Heavenly and Divine,
    Beyond the Common days.

The first Fruits do a Blessing prove
    To all the Sheaves behind.
And they that do a Sabbath love,
    An happy Week shall find.
My Lord on Thee his Name did Fix;
    Which makes thee Rich and Gay.
Amidst these Golden Candlesticks
    My Saviour walks this day.

He walks in's Robes, his Face shines bright;
    The Stars are in his Hand,
Out of his Mouth that place of Might
    A two-edg'd Sword doth stand.
Grac'd with our Lords Appearance thus;
    As well as with his Name,
Thou mayst demand Respect from us
    Upon a double Claim.

This day God doth his Vessels broach;
    His Conduits run with Wine.
He that loves not this Days approach
    Scorns Heaven and Saviour-shine.
What Slaves are those who Slav'ry choose,
    And Garlick for their Feast,
Whilst Milk and Honey they refuse,
    And the Almighty's Rest?

This Market-day doth Saints Enrich
    And smiles upon them all.
It is their *Pentecost*, on which
    The Holy Ghost doth fall.
O Day of Wonders! Mercies Dawn,
    The weary Souls Recruit,
The Christians *Goshen*, Heavens Dawn,
    The Bud of Endless Fruit!

Oh could I love as I have lov'd
    Thy Watches heretofore;
As *England's* Glory thou hast prov'd
    Mayst thou be so yet more.
This day must I for God appear,
    For, Lord, the day is thine.
O let me spend it in thy Fear,
    Then shall the Day be mine.

Cease Work and Play throughout the day,
    That I to God may rest.
Now let me Talk with God, and Walk
    With God, and I am Blest.

A SONG OF PRAISE FOR CHRIST

I've found the Pearl of greatest price.
    My Heart doth Sing for Joy.
And Sing I must. A Christ I have;
    O What a Christ have I!

Christ is the Way, the Truth and Life.
    The Way to God and Glory.
Life to the Dead, the Truth of Types,
    The Truth of Ancient Story.

Christ is a Prophet, Priest and King:
    A Prophet full of Light,
A Priest that stands 'twixt God and Man.
    A King that Rules with Might.
Christ's Manhood is a Temple, where,
    The Altar, God doth Rest.
My Christ, He is the Sacrifice.
    My Christ, He is the Priest.

My Christ, He is the Lord of Lords,
    He is the King of Kings.
He is the Sun of Righteousness
    With Healing in his Wings.
My Christ, He is the Tree of Life
    Which in God's Garden grows,
Whose Fruits do Feed, whose Leaves do Heal,
    My Christ is *Sharons* Rose.

Christ is my Meat, Christ is my Drink,
    My Physick and my Health;
My peace, my Strength, my joy, my Crown,
    My Glory and my Wealth.
Christ is my Father and my Friend,
    My Brother and my Love;
My Head, my Hope, my Counsellour,
    My Advocate above.

My Christ he is the Heaven of Heaven,
    My Christ what shall I call?
My Christ is first, my Christ is last,
    My Christ is All in All.

Spiritual Songs, 1683

THE SINNERS FEARS

Alas! for I have seen the Lord,
    With a drawn Sword he stood,
Now might he sheath it in my flesh,
    And bathe it in my blood;
I've dar'd him with my mighty sins,
    As if he was too slow,
But now he comes both arm'd and girt,
    As an inraged Foe.

What shall a guilty sinner do?
    When Justice do's appear,
Or whither shall I flee from him,
    Whose place is every where?
As I can neither stand nor fly,
    For neither can I bear,
That mighty hand which Grinds the Rocks,
    And doth foundations tear.

My pale, my poor, my trembling Soul
    Do's start at every thing,
It hourly fears huge Hosts of wrath
    From this incensed King;
Should he but his Commissions grant
    All creatures would engage
Against me as their common foe,
    With an united rage.

I have such Monsters in my Soul,
    As do portend and tell,
As Devils here with me have dwelt
    So I with them must dwell;
They have my wretched Soul possest,
    They hold it in their chains,
I fear least they should drag it down
    To suffer endless pains.

My fears are just, I've serv'd for Hell,
    And 'tis my proper Hire,
But who can dwell, O who can dwell
    With everlasting Fire?

THE SINNERS AMAZEMENT

(As the 25 Psalm)

I read that sins are Clouds,
    Whence Vengeance storms have fell,
But this is that, I wonder at,
    That I am out of Hell.
Sure there are those in Hell,
    Who never have deserv'd
In Hell to lie, so much as I,
    And yet I am preserv'd.

My sins have proudly scorn'd,
    My sins have boldly dar'd
The God of Might, with much despight,
    And yet my Soul is spar'd.
The best and goodliest things,
    Which did this World adorn,
By sin are rac't, and quite defac't,
    Yet still I am forborn.

At our first Parents breach,
    Pale Death came rushing in,
The Angels fell from Heav'n to Hell
    Prest with the weights of sin.
The Sodomites Cry prevail'd,
    Hell could no longer stay,
But loe there came a Sulph'rous Flame
    And met them by the way.

When *Corah* did Rebel,
    Earth would not be his Slave,
To bear his weight, but opens streight,
    And was his willing Grave.
When *Israel* did corrupt
    The Air with murmuring breath,
It did rebound, and gave a wound,
    And that was present Death.

The whole Creation groans,
    Sins wracks the World do fill,
It empties Rooms, to furnish Tombs,
    Yet I am living still.
On the Lords hand I live,
    And cannot but admire,
He does not shake so vile a Snake
    Into Eternal Fire.

That Miracles are ceas'd,
    Some confidently tell;
But I do know it is not so,
    Whilst I am out of Hell.

Penitential Cries in Thirty Two Hymns, 1693

Thomas Ken. 1637–1711

A MORNING HYMN

Awake my Soul, and with the Sun,
Thy daily stage of Duty run;
Shake off dull Sloth, and early rise,
To pay Thy Morning Sacrifice.

Redeem Thy mis-spent time that's past;
Live this day, as if 'twere thy last;
T' improve thy talent take due care,
'Gainst the great Day thy self prepare.

Let all thy Converse be sincere,
Thy Conscience as the Noon-day clear,
Think how All-seeing God thy ways,
And all thy secret thoughts surveys.

Influenc'd by the Light divine,
Let thy own light in good works shine:
Reflect all Heaven's propitious ways,
In ardent love, and chearful praise.

Wake, and lift up thy self, my Heart,
And with the Angels bear thy part,
Who all night long Unwearied sing,
Glory to the Eternal King.

I wake, I wake, ye heavenly Choire,
May your Devotion me inspire,
That I like you my Age may spend,
Like you may on my God attend.

May I like you in God delight,
Have all day long my God in sight,
Perform like you my Makers will,
O may I never more do ill.

Had I your Wings to Heaven I'd fly,
But God shall that defect supply,
And my Soul wing'd with warm desire,
Shall all day long to Heav'n aspire.

Glory to Thee who safe hast kept,
And hast refresh't me whilst I slept:
Grant Lord when I from death shall wake,
I may of endless light partake.

I would not wake, not rise again,
Ev'n Heav'n it self I would disdain,
Wer't not Thou there to be enjoy'd,
And I in Hymns to be employ'd.

Heav'n is, dear Lord, where e'er Thou art,
O never then from me depart;
For to my Soul 'tis Hell to be,
But for one moment without Thee.

Lord, I my vows to Thee renew,
Scatter my Sins as Morning dew,
Guard my first springs of thought, and will,
And with Thy self my Spirit fill.

Direct, controul, suggest this day,
All I design, or do, or say;
That all my powers, with all their might,
In thy sole Glory may Unite.

Praise God, from whom all Blessings flow,
Praise him all creatures here below
Praise Him above y'Angelick Host
Praise Father, Son and Holy Ghost.

AN EVENING HYMN

Glory to Thee, my God, this night,
For all the blessings of the light;
Keep me, O keep me King of Kings,
Under thy own Almighty Wings.

Forgive me Lord, for thy dear Son,
The ill that I this day have done,
That with the world, my self, and Thee,
I, e're I sleep, at peace may be.

Teach me to live, that I may dread
The Grave as little as my Bed;
Teach me to die, that so I may
Triumphing rise at the last day.

O may my Soul on thee repose,
And with sweet sleep mine Eye-lids close;
Sleep that may me more vig'rous make,
To serve my God when I awake.

When in the night I sleepless lye,
My Soul with Heavenly thoughts supply,
Let no ill dreams disturb my rest,
No powers of darkness me molest.

Dull sleep of sense me to deprive,
I am but half my days alive;
Thy faithful lovers, Lord, are griev'd,
To lye so long of Thee bereav'd.

But though sleep o're my frailty reigns,
Let it not hold me long in chains;
And now and then let loose my heart,
Till it an Halleluiah dart.

The faster sleep the sense does bind,
The more unfetter'd is the mind;
O may my Soul from matter free,
Thy unvail'd Goodness waking see!

O when shall I in endless day,
For ever chase dark sleep away,
And endless praise with th' Heavenly Choire,
Incessant sing, and never tire?

You, my Blest Guardian, whilst I sleep,
Close to my Bed your Vigills keep,
Divine Love into me instill,
Stop all the avenues of ill.

Thought to thought with my Soul converse,
Celestial joys to me rehearse,
And in my stead all the night long,
Sing to my God a grateful Song.

Praise God from whom all blessings flow,
Praise him all Creatures here below,
Praise him above y' Angelick Host,
Praise Father, Son, and Holy Ghost.

A MIDNIGHT HYMN

Lord, now my Sleep does me forsake,
The sole possession of me take,
Let no vain fancy me illude,
No one impure desire intrude.

Blest Angels! while we silent lye,
You Halleluiahs sing on high,
You, ever wakeful near the Throne,
Prostrate, adore the Three in One.

I now awake do with you joyn,
To praise our God in Hymns divine:
With you in Heav'n I hope to dwell.
And bid the night and world farewel.

My Soul, when I shake off this dust,
Lord, in thy Arms I will entrust;
O make me thy peculiar care,
Some heav'nly Mansion me prepare.

Give me a place at thy Saints feet,
Or some fall'n Angel's vacant seat;
I'll strive to sing as loud as they,
Who sit above in brighter day.

O may I always ready stand,
With my Lamp burning in my hand,
May I in sight of Heav'n rejoyce,
When e're I hear the Bridegrooms voice.

Glory to thee in light array'd,
Who light thy dwelling place hast made,
An immense Ocean of bright beams,
From thy All-glorious Godhead streams.

The Sun in its Meridian height,
Is very darkness in thy sight:
My Soul, O lighten, and enflame,
With Thought and Love of thy great Name.

Blest Jesu, thou on Heav'n intent,
Whole nights hast in Devotion spent,
But I, frail Creature, soon am tir'd,
And all my Zeal is soon expir'd.

My Soul how canst Thou weary grow,
Of Antedating Heav'n below,
In sacred Hymns, and Divine Love,
Which will eternal be above?

Shine on me Lord, new life impart,
Fresh ardours kindle in my heart;
One ray of thy All-quickning light,
Dispels the sloth and clouds of night.

Lord, lest the tempter me surprize,
Watch over thine own Sacrifice,
All loose, all idle thoughts cast out,
And make my very dreams devout.

Praise God from whom all blessings flow,
Praise him all Creatures here below,
Praise him above y'Angelick Host,
Praise Father, Son, and Holy Ghost.

Three Hymns, 1694

Nahum Tate. 1652–1715

&

Nicolas Brady. 1659–1726

PSALM XLII

As pants the Hart for cooling Streams,
    when heated in the Chace,
So longs my Soul, O God, for thee,
    and thy refreshing Grace.
For thee, my God, the living God,
    my thirsty Soul doth pine;
O when shall I behold thy Face,
    thou Majesty Divine!

Tears are my constant Food, while thus
    insulting Foes upbraid,
"Deluded Wretch, where's now thy God?
    "and where his promis'd Aid?
I sigh, when-e'er my musing Thought
    those happy Days present,
When I with Troops of pious Friends
    thy Temple did frequent.

When I advanc'd with Songs of Praise,
    my solemn Vows to pay,
And led the joyful sacred Throng
    that kept the Festal Day.
Why restless, why cast down my Soul?
    trust God, who will employ
His aid for thee; and change these Sighs
    to thankful Hymns of Joy.

My Soul's cast down, O God, but thinks
    on thee, and *Sion* still;

From *Jordan's* Bank, from *Hermon's* Heights,
    and *Missar's* humbler Hill.
One Trouble calls another on,
    and gath'ring o'er my Head,
Fall spouting down, till round my Soul
    a roaring Sea is spread.

But when thy Presence, Lord of Life,
    has once dispell'd this Storm,
To thee I'll midnight Anthems sing,
    and all my Vows perform.
God of my Strength, how long shall I
    like one forgotten mourn?
Forlorn, forsaken, and expos'd
    to my Oppressor's Scorn.

My Heart is pierc'd, as with a Sword,
    whilst thus my Foes upbraid;
"Vain Boaster, where is now thy God?
    "and where his promis'd Aid?
Why restless, why cast down my Soul?
    hope still, and thou shalt sing
The Praise of him who is thy God,
    thy Health's Eternal Spring.

PSALM CXLVIII

Ye boundless Realms of Joy
Exalt your Maker's Fame;
His Praise your Song employ
Above the Starry Frame:
    Your Voices raise,
        Ye Cherubim
        And Seraphim,
    To sing his Praise.

Thou Moon, that rul'st the Night,
And Sun that guid'st the Day,
Ye glitt'ring Stars of Light,
To him your Homage pay:
His Praise declare
Ye Heav'ns above,
And Clouds that move
In liquid Air.

Let them adore the Lord,
And praise his holy Name,
By whose Almighty Word
They all from nothing came;
And all shall last
From Changes free;
His firm Decree
Stand ever fast.

Let Earth her Tribute pay;
Praise him, ye dreadful Whales,
And Fish that thro the Sea
Glide swift with glitt'ring Scales,
Fire, Hail, and Snow,
And misty Air,
And winds that, where
He bids them, blow.

By Hills and Mountains (all
In grateful Consort join'd)
By Cedars stately tall,
And Trees for Fruit design'd:
By ev'ry Beast,
And creeping thing,
And Fowl of Wing
His Name be blest.

Let all of Royal Birth,
With those of humbler Frame;
And Judges of the Earth,
His matchless Praise proclaim.
 In this Design
  Let Youths with Maids,
  And hoary Heads
 With Children join.

United Zeal be shown,
His wond'rous Fame to raise,
Whose glorious Name alone
Deserves our endless Praise.
 Earth's utmost Ends
  His Pow'r obey:
  His glorious Sway
 The Sky transcends.

His chosen Saints to grace
He sets them up on high,
And favours *Israel's* Race
Who still to him are nigh.
 O therefore raise
  Your grateful voice
  And still rejoice
 The Lord to praise.

A New Version of the Psalms of David, 1699

SONG OF THE ANGELS AT THE NATIVITY OF OUR

BLESSED SAVIOUR

Luke ii from v. 8 to v. 15.

While Shepherds watch'd their Flocks by Night
 all seated on the Ground,
The Angel of the Lord came down,
 and Glory shone around.

"Fear not, said he, (for mighty Dread
    "had seiz'd their troubled Mind)
"Glad Tidings of great Joy I bring
    "to you and all Mankind;

"To you, in *David's* Town this Day
    "is born of *David's* Line,
"The Saviour, who is Christ the Lord;
    "and this shall be the sign:
"The heav'nly Babe you there shall find
    "to humane view display'd,
"All meanly wrapt in swathing Bands,
    "and in a Manger laid.

Thus spake the Seraph, and forthwith
    appear'd a shining Throng
Of Angels praising God, and thus
    addrest their joyful Song;
"All Glory be to God on high,
    "and to the Earth be Peace;
"Good-will, henceforth, from Heav'n to Men,
    "begin and never cease.

A Supplement to the New Version, 1700

Joseph Addison. 1672–1719

The Spacious Firmament on high,
With all the blue Etherial Sky,
And spangled Heav'ns, a Shining Frame,
Their great Original proclaim:
Th'unwearied Sun, from day to day,
Does his Creator's Pow'r display,
And publishes to every Land
The Work of an Almighty Hand.

Soon as the Evening Shades prevail,
The Moon takes up the wondrous Tale,
And nightly to the listning Earth
Repeats the Story of her Birth:
Whilst all the Stars that round her burn,
And all the Planets, in their turn,
Confirm the Tidings as they rowl,
And spread the Truth from Pole to Pole.

What though, in solemn Silence, all
Move round the dark terrestrial Ball?
What tho' nor real Voice nor Sound
Amid their radiant Orbs be found?
In Reason's Ear they all rejoice,
And utter forth a glorious Voice,
For ever singing, as they shine,
The Hand that made us is Divine.

The Spectator, 23 August 1712

ISAAC WATTS AND HIS FOLLOWERS
1709–1787

Isaac Watts. 1674–1748

CONDESCENDING GRACE
In Imitation of the 114th Psalm

When the Eternal bows the Skies
    To visit Earthly Things,
With Scorn divine he turns his Eyes
    From Towers of haughty Kings;

Rides on a Cloud disdainful by
    A *Sultan* or a *Czar*,
Laughs at the Worms that rise so high,
    Or frowns 'em from afar;

He bids his awful Chariot roll
    Far downward from the Skies
To visit every humble Soul
    With Pleasure in his Eyes.

Why should the Lord that reigns above
    Disdain so lofty Kings?
Say, Lord, and why such Looks of Love
    Upon such worthless things?

Mortals, be dumb; what Creature dares
    Dispute his awful Will?
Ask no Account of his Affairs,
    But tremble and be still.

Just like his Nature is his Grace,
    All Sovereign and all free;
Great God, how searchless are thy Ways?
    How deep thy Judgments be?

THE HAZARD OF LOVING THE CREATURES

Where e'er my flatt'ring Passions rove
    I find a lurking Snare;
'Tis dangerous to let loose our Love
    Beneath th' Eternal Fair.

Souls whom the Tye of Friendship binds,
    And Partners of our Blood,
Seize a large Portion of our Minds,
    And leave the less for God.

Nature has soft but powerful Bands,
    And Reason she controuls;
While Children with their little Hands
    Hang closest to our Souls.

Thoughtless they act th' old Serpents Part;
    What tempting things they be!
Lord, how they twine about our Heart,
    And draw it off from thee!

Our hasty Wills rush blindly on
    Where rising Passion rolls,
And thus we make our Fetters strong
    To bind our slavish Souls,

Dear Sovereign, break these Fetters off,
    And set our Spirits free;
God in himself is Bliss enough,
    For we have all in thee.

Horae Lyricae, 1709

DIVINE WRATH AND MERCY

from Nahum i. 1, 2, 3, &c.

*Heb. 12. 29.

Adore and tremble, for our God
 Is a *Consuming Fire*,
His jealous Eyes his Wrath enflame,
 And raise his Vengeance higher.

Almighty Vengeance how it burns!
 How bright his Fury glows!
Vast Magazines of Plagues and Storms
 Lie treasur'd for his Foes.

Those heaps of Wrath by slow degrees
 Are forc'd into a Flame,
But kindled, oh! how fierce they blaze!
 And rend all Nature's Frame.

At his Approach the Mountains flee,
 And seek a watry Grave;
The frighted Sea makes hast away,
 And shrinks up every wave.

Through the wide Air the weighty Rocks
 Are swift as Hail-stones hurl'd:
Who dares engage his fiery Rage
 That shakes the Solid World?

Yet Mighty God, thy Sovereign Grace
 Sits Regent on the Throne,
The Refuge of thy chosen Race
 When Wrath comes rushing down.

Thy Hand shall on Rebellious Kings
 A fiery Tempest pour.
While we beneath thy shelt'ring Wings
 Thy Just Revenge adore.

BABYLON FALLEN
Rev. xviii. 20, 21.

In *Gabriel's* Hand a Mighty Stone
Lyes, a fair Type of *Babylon*:
Prophets rejoyce, and all ye Saints,
God shall avenge your long Complaints.

He said, and dreadful as he stood,
He sunk the Milstone in the Flood:
Thus terribly shall Babel *fall,*
Thus, and no more be found at all.

PARTING WITH CARNAL JOYS

I send the Joys of Earth away,
Away ye Tempters of the Mind,
False as the smooth deceitful Sea,
And empty as the whistling Wind.

Your Streams were floating me along
Down to the Gulph of black Despair,
And whilst I listen'd to your Song,
Your Streams had e'en convey'd me there.

Lord, I adore thy matchless Grace,
That warn'd me of that dark Abyss,
That drew me from those treacherous Seas,
And bid me seek superiour Bliss.

Now to the shining Realms above
I stretch my Hands, and glance mine Eyes,
O for the Pinions of a Dove,
To bear me to the upper Skies!

There from the Bosom of my God
Oceans of endless Pleasure roll,
There would I fix my last Abode,
And drown the Sorrows of my Soul.

COMPLAINING OF SPIRITUAL SLOTH

My drowzie Powers, why sleep ye so?
    Awake my sluggish Soul!
Nothing has half thy Work to do,
    Yet nothing's half so dull.

The little Ants for one poor Grain
    Labour, and tugg, and strive,
Yet we who have a Heaven t' obtain
    How negligent we live!

We for whose sake all Nature stands,
    And Stars their Courses move;
We for whose Guard the Angel-bands
    Come flying from above;

We for whom God the Son came down,
    And labour'd for our Good,
How careless to secure that Crown
    He purchas'd with his Blood?

Lord, shall we lie so sluggish still,
    And never act our Parts?
Come, holy Dove, from th' heav'nly Hill,
    And sit and warm our Hearts.

Then shall our active Spirits move,
    Upward our Souls shall rise:
With Hands of Faith and Wings of Love
    We'll fly and take the Prize.

GOD INVISIBLE

Lord, we are blind, we Mortals blind,
We can't behold thy bright Abode;
O 'tis beyond a Creature Mind,
To glance a Thought half way to God.

Infinite Leagues beyond the Sky
The Great Eternal reigns alone,
Where neither Wings nor Souls can fly,
Nor Angels climb the topless Throne.

The Lord of Glory builds his Seat
Of Gems insufferably bright,
And lays beneath his sacred Feet
Substantial Beams of gloomy Night.

Yet, glorious Lord, thy gracious Eyes
Look thro', and chear us from above;
Beyond our Praise thy Grandeur flies,
Yet we adore, and yet we love.

A SIGHT OF GOD MORTIFIES US TO THE WORLD

[Up to the Fields where Angels lye,
And living Waters gently roll,
Fain would my Thoughts leap out and fly,
But Sin hangs heavy on my Soul.

Thy wondrous Blood, dear dying *Christ*,
Can make this load of Guilt remove;
And thou canst bear me where thou fly'st,
On thy kind Wings, Celestial Dove.]

O might I once mount up and see
The Glories of th' Eternal Skies,
What little things these Worlds would be,
How despicable to my Eyes!

Had I a Glance of thee, my God,
Kingdoms and Men would vanish soon,
Vanish as tho' I saw 'em not,
As a dim Candle dies at Noon.

Then they might fight, and rage, and rave,
I should perceive the Noise no more
Than we can hear a shaking Leaf
While rattling Thunders round us roar.

Great All in All, Eternal King,
Let me but view thy lovely Face,
And all my Pow'rs shall bow and sing,
Thine endless Grandeur, and thy Grace.

THE HOPE OF HEAVEN OUR SUPPORT UNDER TRIALS ON EARTH

When I can read my Title clear
    To Mansions in the Skies,
I bid farewel to every Fear,
    And wipe my weeping Eyes.

Should Earth against my Soul engage,
    And hellish Darts be hurl'd,
Then I can smile at *Satan's* Rage,
    And face a frowning World.

Let Cares like a wild Deluge come,
    And Storms of Sorrow fall,
May I but safely reach my Home,
    My God, my Heaven, my All.

There shall I bathe my weary Soul
 In Seas of heavenly Rest;
And not a Wave of Trouble roll,
 Across my peaceful Breast.

A PROSPECT OF HEAVEN MAKES DEATH EASY

There is a Land of pure Delight
 Where Saints Immortal reign;
Infinite Day excludes the Night,
 And Pleasures banish Pain.

There everlasting Spring abides,
 And never-withering Flowers:
Death like a narrow Sea divides
 This Heav'nly Land from ours.

[Sweet Fields beyond the swelling Flood
 Stand drest in living Green:
So to the *Jews* old *Canaan* stood,
 While *Jordan* roll'd between.

But timorous Mortals start and shrink
 To cross this narrow Sea,
And linger shivering on the Brink,
 And fear to lanch away.]

O could we make our Doubts remove,
 These gloomy Doubts that rise,
And see the *Canaan* that we love,
 With unbeclouded Eyes.

Could we but climb where *Moses* stood,
 And view the Landskip o're,
Not *Jordan's* Stream, nor Death's cold Flood,
 Should fright us from the Shore.

93

ANGELS MINISTRING TO CHRIST AND SAINTS

The Majesty of *Solomon*!
   How glorious to behold
The Servants waiting round his Throne,
   The Ivory and the Gold!

But, mighty God, thy Palace shines
   With far superiour Beams:
Thine Angel-Guards are swift as Winds,
   Thy Ministers are Flames.

[Soon as thine only Son had made
   His Entrance on this Earth,
A shining Army downward fled
   To celebrate his Birth.

And when opprest with Pains and Fears
   On the cold Ground he lies,
Behold a heav'nly Form appears
   T'allay his Agonies.]

Now to the Hands of *Christ* our King
   Are all their Legions giv'n;
They wait upon his Saints, and bring
   His chosen Heirs to Heaven.

Pleasure and Praise run thro' their Host
   To see a Sinner turn;
Then *Satan* has a Captive lost,
   And *Christ* a Subject born.

But there's an Hour of brighter Joy
   When he his Angels sends
Obstinate Rebels to destroy,
   And gather in his Friends.

O could I say, without a Doubt,
　　There shall my Soul be found,
Then let the great Archangel shout,
　　And the last Trumpet sound.

THE VANITY OF CREATURES; OR, NO REST ON EARTH

Man has a Soul of vast Desires
He burns within with restless Fires,
Tost to and fro his Passions fly
From Vanity to Vanity.

In vain on Earth we hope to find
Some solid Good to fill the Mind,
We try new Pleasures, but we feel
The inward Thirst and Torment still.

So when a raging Fever burns
We shift from side to side by turns,
And 'tis a poor Relief we gain
To change the Place, but keep the Pain.

Great God subdue this vicious Thirst,
This Love to Vanity and Dust;
Cure the vile Fever of the Mind,
And feed our Souls with Joys refin'd.

CUSTOM IN SIN

Let the wild *Leopards* of the Wood
Put off the Spots that Nature gives,
Then may the Wicked turn to God,
And change their Tempers, and their Lives.

As well might *Ethiopian* slaves
Wash out the Darkness of their Skin;
The Dead as well may leave their Graves
As Old Trangressors cease to sin.

Where Vice has held its Empire long
'Twill not indure the least Controll;
None but a Power divinely strong
Can turn the Current of the Soul.

Great God, I own thy Power Divine,
That works to change this Heart of mine;
I would be form'd anew, and bless
The Wonders of Creating Grace.

CRUCIFIXION TO THE WORLD BY THE CROSS OF CHRIST

Gal. vi. 14

When I survey the wondrous Cross
On which the Prince of Glory dy'd,
My richest Gain I count but Loss,
And pour Contempt on all my Pride.

Forbid it, Lord, that I should boast
Save in the Death of *Christ* my God;
All the vain things that charm me most,
I sacrifice them to his Blood.

See from his Head, his Hands, his Feet,
Sorrow and Love flow mingled down;
Did e'er such Love and Sorrow meet?
Or Thorns compose so rich a Crown?

[His dying Crimson like a Robe
Spreads o'er his Body on the Tree,
Then am I dead to all the Globe,
And all the Globe is dead to me.]

Were the whole Realm of Nature mine,
That were a Present far too small;
Love so amazing, so divine
Demands my Soul, my Life, my All.

Hymns and Spiritual Songs, 1716

PRAISE FOR MERCIES SPIRITUAL AND TEMPORAL

Whene'er I take my Walks abroad,
How many Poor I see?
What shall I render to my God
For all his Gifts to me?

Not more than others I deserve,
Yet God hath giv'n me more;
For I have Food while others starve,
Or beg from Door to Door.

How many Children in the Street
Half naked I behold?
While I am cloth'd from Head to Feet,
And cover'd from the Cold.

While some poor Wretches scarce can tell
Where they may lay their Head,
I have a Home wherein to dwell,
And rest upon my Bed.

While others early learn to swear,
And curse, and lye, and steal,
Lord, I am taught thy Name to fear,
And do thy holy Will.

Are these thy Favours Day by Day
To me above the rest?
Then let me love thee more than they,
And try to serve thee best.

AGAINST QUARRELLING AND FIGHTING

Let Dogs delight to bark and bite,
　　For God has made them so;
Let Bears and Lions growl and fight,
　　For 'tis their Nature too.

But Children, you should never let
　　Such angry Passions rise;
Your little Hands were never made
　　To tear each others Eyes.

Let Love thro' all your Actions run,
　　And all your Words be mild,
Live like the blessed Virgin's Son,
　　That Sweet and lovely Child.

His Soul was gentle as a Lamb;
　　And as his Stature grew,
He grew in Favour both with Man,
　　And God his Father too.

Now Lord of all he reigns above,
　　And from his heav'nly Throne,
He sees what Children dwell in Love,
　　And marks them for his own.

AGAINST IDLENESS AND MISCHIEF

How doth the little busy Bee
　　Improve each shining Hour,
And gather Honey all the Day
　　From ev'ry op'ning Flow'r!

How skilfully she builds her Cell!
    How neat she spreads the Wax;
And labours hard to store it well
    With the sweet Food she makes.

In Works of Labour or of Skill
    I would be busy too:
For *Satan* finds some Mischief still
    For idle Hands to do.

In Books, or Work, or healthful Play
    Let my first Years be past,
That I may give for every Day
    Some good Account at last.

AGAINST PRIDE IN CLOTHES

Why should our Garments (made to hide
Our Parents Shame) provoke our Pride?
The Art of Dress did ne'er begin,
'Till *Eve* our Mother learnt to sin.

When first she put her Cov'ring on,
Her Robe of Innocence was gone:
And yet her Children vainly boast
In the sad Marks of Glory lost.

How proud we are! how fond to shew
Our Clothes, and call them rich and new!
When the poor Sheep and Silk-worm wore
That very Cloathing long before.

The Tulip and the Butterfly
Appear in gayer Coats than I:
Let me be drest fine as I will,
Flies, Worms, and Flowers exceed me still.

Then will I set my Heart to find
Inward Adornings of the Mind;
Knowledge and Virtue, Truth and Grace,
These are the Robes of richest Dress.

No more shall Worms with me compare;
This is the Rayment Angels wear:
The Son of God, when here below,
Put on this blest Apparel too.

It never fades, it ne'er grows old,
Nor fears the Rain, nor Moth, nor Mould;
It takes no Spot, but still refines;
The more 'tis worn, the more it shines.

In this on Earth would I appear,
Then go to Heaven, and wear it there:
God will approve it in his Sight,
'Tis his own Work, and his Delight.

A CRADLE HYMN

Hush! my Dear, lie still and slumber;
Holy Angels guard thy Bed!
Heavenly Blessings without Number
Gently falling on thy Head.

Sleep my Babe; thy Food and Rayment,
House and Home thy Friends provide;
All without thy Care or Payment,
All thy Wants are well supply'd.

How much better thou'rt attended
Than the *Son of God* could be,
When from Heaven he descended
And became a Child like thee.

Soft and easy is thy Cradle;
Coarse and hard thy Saviour lay,
When his Birth-Place was a Stable,
And his softest Bed was Hay.

Blessed Babe! what glorious Features
Spotless fair, divinely bright!
Must he dwell with brutal Creatures?
How could Angels bear the Sight?

Was there nothing but a Manger
Cursed sinners could afford,
To receive the heavenly Stranger?
Did they thus affront their Lord?

Soft, my Child; I did not chide thee,
Tho' my Song might sound too hard:
'Tis thy $\begin{Bmatrix} \text{*Mother} \\ \text{Nurse that} \end{Bmatrix}$ sits beside thee,
And her Arm shall be thy Guard.

Yet to read the shameful Story
How the *Jews* abus'd their King,
How they serv'd the *Lord of Glory*,
Makes me angry while I sing.

See the kinder Shepherds round him,
Telling Wonders from the Skie;
There they sought him, there they found him,
With his Virgin-Mother by.

See the lovely Babe a dressing;
Lovely Infant how he smil'd!
When he wept, the Mother's Blessing
Sooth'd and hush'd the holy Child.

* Here you may use the words, *Brother, Sister, Neighbour, Friend, &c.*

Lo, he slumbers in his Manger,
Where the horned Oxen fed;
Peace, my Darling, here's no Danger,
Here's no Ox anear thy Bed.

'Twas to save thee, Child, from dying,
Save my Dear from burning Flame,
Bitter Groans, and endless Crying,
That thy blest Redeemer came.

May'st thou live to know and fear him,
Trust and love him all thy Days!
Then go dwell for ever near him,
See his Face, and sing his Praise!

I could give thee thousand Kisses,
Hoping what I most desire:
Not a Mother's fondest wishes,
Can to greater Joys aspire.

Divine Songs Attempted in easy language, for the Use of Children,
1728

CHRIST'S KINGDOM AMONG THE GENTILES

Psalm lxii. Second Part

Jesus shall reign where e'er the Sun
Does his successive Journeys run;
His Kingdom stretch from Shore to Shore,
Till Moons shall wax and wane no more.

[Behold the Islands with their Kings,
And *Europe* her best Tribute brings;
From *North to South* the Princes meet
To pay their Homage at his Feet.

There *Persia* glorious to behold,
There *India* shines in *Eastern* Gold;
And barbarous Nations at his Word
Submit and bow and own their Lord.]

For him shall endless Pray'r be made,
And Praises throng to crown his Head;
His Name like sweet Perfume shall rise
With every Morning Sacrifice.

People and Realms of every Tongue
Dwell on his Love with sweetest Song;
And Infant-Voices shall proclaim
Their early Blessings on his Name.

Blessings abound where e'er he reigns,
The Prisoner leaps to lose his Chains,
The Weary find eternal Rest,
And all the Sons of Want are blest.

[Where he displays his healing Power,
Death and the Curse are known no more;
In him the Tribes of *Adam* boast
More Blessings than their Father lost.

Let every Creature rise and bring,
Peculiar Honours to our King:
Angels descend with Songs again,
And Earth repeat the long *Amen.*]

MAN FRAIL AND GOD ETERNAL

Psalm xc. 1–5. First Part

Our God, our Help in Ages past,
    Our Hope for Years to come,
Our Shelter from the stormy Blast,
    And our eternal Home.

Under the Shadow of thy Throne
    Thy Saints have dwelt secure;
Sufficient is thine Arm alone,
    And our Defence is sure.

Before the Hills in order stood,
    Or Earth receiv'd her Frame,
From everlasting Thou art God,
    To endless Years the same.

Thy Word commands our Flesh to Dust,
    Return, ye Sons of Men:
All Nations rose from Earth at first,
    And turn to Earth again.

A thousand Ages in thy Sight
    Are like an Evening gone;
Short as the Watch that ends the Night
    Before the rising Sun.

[The busy Tribes of Flesh and Blood
    With all their Lives and Cares
Are carried downwards by thy Flood,
    And lost in following Years.

Time like an ever rolling Stream
    Bears all its Sons away;
They fly forgotten as a Dream
    Dies at the opening Day.

Like flow'ry Fields the Nations stand
    Pleas'd with the Morning-light;
The Flowers beneath the Mower's Hand
    Lie withering e'er 'tis Night.]

Our God, our Help in Ages Past,
    Our Hope for Years to come,
Be thou our Guard while Troubles last,
    And our eternal Home.

The Psalms of David, 1719

Philip Doddridge. 1702–1751

COMMUNING WITH OUR HEARTS

Psalm iv. 4

Return, my roving heart, return,
And chase these shadowy forms no more;
Seek out some solitude to mourn,
And thy forsaken God implore.

Wisdom and pleasure dwell at home;
Retired and silent seek them there;
True conquest is ourselves to o'ercome,—
True strength to break the tempter's snare.

And thou, my God, whose piercing eye
Distinct surveys each deep recess,
In these abstracted hours draw nigh,
And with thy presence fill the place.

Through all the mazes of my heart
My search let heavenly wisdom guide,
And still its radiant beams impart,
Till all be search'd, and purified.

Then, with the visits of thy love,
Vouchsafe my trembling soul to cheer;
Till every grace shall join to prove,
That God hath fix'd his dwelling there.

CHRIST SANCTIFYING HIMSELF, THAT HIS PEOPLE MAY BE SANCTIFIED

John. xvii. 1.19

Behold the bleeding Lamb of God,
    Our spotless sacrifice!
By hands of barbarous sinners seized,
    Nail'd to the cross he dies.

Blest Jesus, whence this streaming blood?
    And whence this foul disgrace?
Whence all these pointed thorns, that rend
    Thy venerable face?

"I sanctify myself," he cries,
    "That thou mayst holy be;
Come trace my life; come, view my death,
    And learn to copy me."

Dear Lord, we pant for holiness,
    And inbred sin we mourn:
To the bright path of thy commands
    Our wandering footsteps turn.

Not more sincerely would we wish
    To climb the heavenly hill,
Than here with all our utmost power
    Thy wishes to fulfil.

MEDITATIONS ON THE SEPULCHRE IN THE GARDEN

John. xix. 41

The Sepulchres, how thick they stand
Through all the road on either hand!
And burst upon our starting sight
In every garden of delight!

Thither the winding alleys tend;
There all the flowery borders end;
And forms, that charm'd our eyes before,
Fragrance and beauty are no more.

Deep in the grave's damp silent cell
My fathers and my brethren dwell;
Beneath its deep and gloomy shade
My kindred and my friends are laid.

But, while I tread the solemn way,
My faith that Saviour would survey,
Who deign'd to sojourn in the tomb,
And left behind a rich perfume.

My thoughts with ecstasy unknown,
While from his grave they view his throne,
Through my own sepulchre can see
A paradise reserved for me.

VICTORY OVER SATAN BY THE BLOOD OF THE LAMB,
AND THE WORD OF THE TESTIMONY OF HIS SERVANTS

Revelation xii. 11

See the old Dragon from his throne
Sink with enormous ruin down!
Banish'd from heaven, and doom'd to dwell
Deep in the fiery gloom of hell!

Ye heavens with all your hosts, rejoice;
Ye saints, in consort lend your voice:
Approach your Lord's victorious seat,
And tread the foe beneath your feet.

But whence a conquest so divine
Gain'd by such feeble hands as mine?
Or whence can sinful mortals boast
O'er Satan and his rebel-host?

'Twas from thy blood, thou slaughter'd Lamb,
That all our palms and triumphs came;
Thy cross thy spear, inflicts the stroke,
By which the monster's head is broke.

Thy faithful word our hope maintains
Through all our combat and our pains;
The accents of thy heavenly breath
Thy soldiers bear through wounds and death.

Triumphant Lamb, in worlds unknown,
With transport round thy radiant throne,
Thy happy legions, all complete,
Shall lay their laurels at thy feet.

Scriptural Hymns, 1839

Anonymous

EXCEEDING GREAT AND PRECIOUS PROMISES

2 Pet. iii. 4

How firm a Foundation, ye Saints of the Lord,
Is laid for your Faith in his excellent Word;
What more can he say than to you he hath said?
You, who unto JESUS for Refuge have fled.

In every Condition, in Sickness, in Health,
In Poverty's Vale, or abounding in Wealth;
At Home and Abroad, on the Land on the Sea,
"As thy Days may demand, shall thy Strength ever be.

"Fear not, I am with thee, O be not dismay'd,
"I, I am thy GOD, and will still give thee Aid;
"I'll strengthen thee, help thee, and cause thee to stand,
"Upheld by my righteous omnipotent Hand.

"When thro' the deep Waters I call thee to go,
"The Rivers of Woe shall not thee overflow;
"For I will be with thee, thy Troubles to bless,
"And sanctify to thee, thy deepest Distress.

"When thro' fiery Trials thy Pathway shall lie,
"My Grace all sufficient shall be thy Supply;
"The Flame shall not hurt thee, I only design
"Thy Dross to consume, and thy Gold to refine.

"Even down to old Age, all my People shall prove
"My Sovereign, eternal, unchangeable Love;
"And when hoary Hairs shall their Temples adorn,
"Like lambs they shall still in my bosom be borne.

"The Soul that on JESUS hath lean'd for Repose,
"*I will not, I will not* desert to his Foes;
"That Soul, tho' all Hell should endeavour to shake,
"*I'll never—no never*—no never forsake*."

* Agreeable to Dr. Doddridge's Translation of Heb. xiii. 5.

A Selection of Hymns from the Best Authors, Intended to be an Appendix to Dr. Watt's Psalms and Hymns, ed. John Rippon, 1787

MINOR SECTS PART I
1726–1754

David Culy. ?–1725

My Lord, my God, why art thou Silent
    Unto my Praise? and like a Giant
Hast broken me both Night and Day?
    I am not able to endure
If thou thy Hand dost not delay.

The more I sigh the more I am seized,
    The more I pray the more amazed,
Why thou should delay thy Help so long,
    My God, my Strength, I'm waiting for it
With such Desires, Death's not so strong.

I am like those that's in a Prison,
    Fast fetter'd, waiting for a Season,
For Liberty, or some Release,
    So in my Laughter I have Sorrow,
My Joys all end in Heaviness.

I am swallow'd daily in an Ocean
    Of Sorrow, which is yet my Portion;
Yet such deep Sorrows too I have,
    All others to it I compare,
I find that mine is cruel as the Grave.

O Lord, how long wilt thou prolong?
    My Sighs they are not hid from thee,
How will it be e'er thou please
    To grant me that which I desire?
To fetch me home and give me Ease?

I still see, my Lord, thou art resolv'd
    Whilst I am here and undissolv'd,
Me of my Joys thou wilt bereave
    With heavy Strokes, to bring me softly
With Bitterness unto the Grave.

If so, why am I yet aspiring?
    I'll chuse, and am desiring
Thou wouldst me slay quite out of hand;
    Why did my Mother's Knees prevent me?
Why did I see the living Land?

The mournful Turtle is my Fellow,
    I chatter like a *Crane* or *Swallow*,
I am longing for the Morning Light
    In Shadows and in gloomy Places,
I brood my Sorrows *Sparrow* like.

If I would tell my Grief to any,
    I know not one amongst a many,
Who can my Sorrows well comprize,
    Yet in my Grief this one thing chears me.
My Lord with me doth sympathize.

I oft in Songs breath out my Sorrow,
    But yet I feel my Heart too narrow
For to express the Grief I have,
    Must Grief be always my Attendance?
And my Companion to the Grave?

        *   *   *

Now we afresh has eat Christ's Flesh,
    Not raw, but throughly boil'd,
Not sod, nor unapprov'd to God,
    In whom he's reconcil'd.

III

God tasted first of that Lamb roast,
    The Priest has offered,
He likes the Smell and Savour well,
    This is our Father's Bread.

He sees not meet two Boards to keep,
    His Children must draw nigh,
His Son's his Lot, whom he begot,
    These are his Family.

We have eat this Bread, as he's our Head,
    In whom all Wrath is spent,
But's rose again, and loos'd Death's Pain,
    This is the thing that's meant.

Father, this Wine and Cup is thine,
    In which thou thinkest good,
To seal to us thou hast no Curse,
    Thou giv'st us Unions Blood.

We can't forget the Benefit
    We have from this Sacrifice,
His Death to us is precious,
    We do it solemnize.

Until he come this shall be done
    For a Memorial,
We are his Mate, we'll celebrate
    His Death and Funeral.

Thou can't deny Society,
    Which we have had with thee,
This we alledge, thou'st left thy Pledge,
    Thy Seal and Signet see.

One Flesh we feed, that's Meat indeed,
　　And Blood which justify,
As sure as spilt we have no Guilt
　　No Sin thou canst espy.

The Works of Mr. David Culy, 1726

THE MORAVIANS

Anonymous

Chicken blessed and caressed, Little Bee on Jesu's Breast;
From the Hurry and the Flurry Of this Earth thou'rt now at
rest: From our Care in lower Regions, Thou art taken to the
Legions Who 'bove human Griefs are rais'd; There thou'rt
kept, the Lamb be prais'd! Chicken blessed, Bee caressed!
Thou that sleep'st on Jesu's Breast.

*　　*　　*

Tune: *What does a Bird, &c.*

So Side-ward looking constantly, So Side-Hole Homesick-
feelingly, Lamb's Heart to creep thro' so intent, So smelling
for the Lamb's Sweat's Scent, On the Magnetick Side, So like
a Drop of Jesu's Sweat, So quiv'ring with Love's Ague sweet,
Like th' Infant leaping*, So drawing Breath in Corpse's Air,
So spouting forth Wounds Moisture clear, So from Grave's
Vapours in a Dew, So panting the Son's Sign to view, Which
Salem's Streets will brighten, When Suns can no more lighten.
Mean while So Lamb-like happily, So Dovelike, and so
Childlikely, with Sinner-Shame so inly red, So like a Sinner
playfull, glad, While in the heart does hum *Efflavit animum*;†

* Luke i. 41, 44.
† *Jesus gave up the Ghost.*

113

Thro' Cross's Joy to weep so prone, So quite in Breast-Plate
Scholars Tone, Like *John* the Fav'rite; So fashion'd to the slain
Lamb's Heart, Like the Child Jesus in each Part, So like dear
Mary Magdalene, Child, Virgin, Marriage-like in one, The Lamb
shall keep his Bride's Soul, Till she can kiss his Side's Hole.

*A Collection of Hymns: consisting chiefly of translations from the
German Hymn-Book of the Moravian Brethen, 1749*

We greet each other in the Side
    Of our beloved Spouse,
Which is ordained for his dear Bride
    Her everlasting House.
The Lamb, the Husband of our hearts,
Hath got, 'tis true, more wounded Parts,
Yet is the bleeding lovely Side
The Chamber of the Bride.

Our Husband's Side-wound is indeed
    The Queen of all his Wounds;
On this the little Pidgeons feed,
    Whom Cross's Air surrounds.
There they fly in and out and sing,
Side's Blood is seen on ev'ry wing,
The bill that picks the Side-hole's floor,
Is red of Blood all o'er.

There sings the little happy croud,
    Warbling their blood-wash'd throats,
No other Bird however proud
    Can imitate their Notes.
They sing their *Pleuræ gloria*!
And to the Lamb *Victoria*!
Amen and Amen sings the choir,
Then flies in to respire.

Blest Flock in th' Cross's Atmosphere,
    You smell of Jesu's Grave,
The Vapours of his Corpse so dear
    Are the Perfume you have.
Its Scent is penetrant and sweet!
When you each other kiss and greet,
This Scent discovers that you were
To Jesu's Body near.

With thy Side's Blood quite cover me,
    And wet me thro' and thro';
For this I pant incessantly,
    And nothing else will do.
The Blood-Sweat in thy Agony
Come in full heat all over me,
Thy Body stretch its breadth and length
O'er me, and give me strength,

A bird that dives into the Side,
    Goes down quite to the Ground,
And finds a Bottom large and wide
    In this so lovely Wound.
A Side-hole's diver will I be:
O Side-hole! I will sink in thee.
My Soul and Body, enter thou
Into the *Pleura* now.

To live and work and sleep therein,
    I'm heartily inclin'd:
As a poor Dove myself to screen,
    Is my whole heart and mind.
O precious Side-hole's cavity!
I want to Spend my Life in thee.
Glory to thee for thy Side-hole,
Dear Husband of my Soul!

115

With all my heart I bow and bend
 Before thy bleeding Feet:
Yet to thy Side I re-ascend,
 Which is to me most sweet.
There in one Side-hole's Joy divine,
I'll spend all future Days of mine.
Yes, yes, I will for ever sit
There, where thy Side was split.

Ye Cross's-air birds, swell the notes
 Of the sweet Side-hole Song,
That Fountain's Juice will clear your throats,
 And help to hold it long.
Each Day and Year shall higher raise
The Side-hole's glory, love and praise:
Hallelujah! Hallelujah!
To the Side *Gloria!*

A Collection of Hymns of the Children of God in all Ages, 1754

CHARLES WESLEY:
HIS CONTEMPORARIES AND FOLLOWERS
1739–1798

Charles Wesley. 1707–1788

ON THE CONVERSION OF A COMMON HARLOT

*There is Joy in the Presence of the Angels of GOD over one Sinner
that repenteth.*—Luke xv. 10.

Sing ye Heavens, and Earth rejoice,
Make to GOD a chearful Noise;
He the Work alone hath done,
He hath glorified his Son.

Sons of GOD exulting rise,
Join the Triumph of the Skies,
See the Prodigal is come,
Shout to bear the Wanderer Home!

Strive in Joy, with Angels strive,
Dead She was, but now's alive,
Loud repeat the glorious Sound,
Lost She was, but now is found!

This thro' Ages all along,
This be still the joyous Song,
Wide diffus'd o'er Earth abroad,
Music in the Ears of GOD.

Rescu'd from the Fowler's Snare,
JESUS spreads his Arms for Her,
JESU'S Arms her sacred Fence:
Come, ye Fiends, and pluck Her thence!

Thence She never shall remove,
Safe in his redeeming Love:
This the Purchase of his Groans!
This the Soul He died for once!

Now the gracious Father smiles,
Now the Saviour boasts his Spoils:
Now the Spirit grieves no more:
Sing ye Heavens, and Earth adore!

HYMN FOR CHRISTMAS-DAY

Hark how all the Welkin rings,
"Glory to the King of Kings,
"Peace on Earth, and Mercy mild,
"GOD and Sinners reconcil'd!

Joyful all ye Nations rise,
Join the Triumph of the Skies,
Universal Nature say
"CHRIST the LORD is born To-day!

CHRIST, by highest Heaven ador'd,
CHRIST, the everlasting LORD,
Late in Time behold Him come,
Offspring of a Virgin's Womb.

Veil'd in Flesh the Godhead see,
Hail th' incarnate Deity!
Pleas'd as Man with Men t'appear,
JESUS our *Immanuel* here.

Hail the heavenly Prince of Peace!
Hail the Sun of Righteousness!
Light and Life to all He brings,
Ris'n with Healing in his Wings.

Mild He lays his Glory by;
Born; that Man no more may die:
Born; to raise the Sons of Earth:
Born; to give them second Birth.

Come, Desire of Nations, come,
Fix in us thy humble Home,
Rise, the Woman's conqu'ring Seed,
Bruise in us the Serpent's Head.

Now display thy saving Power,
Ruin'd Nature now restore,
Now in mystic Union join
Thine to ours, and ours to Thine.

Adam's Likeness, LORD, efface,
Stamp thy Image in its Place,
Second *Adam* from above,
Reinstate us in thy Love.

Let us Thee, tho' lost, regain,
Thee, the Life, the heavenly Man;
O to All Thyself impart,
Form'd in each believing Heart!

A MORNING HYMN

CHRIST, whose Glory fills the Skies,
    CHRIST, the true, the only Light,
Sun of Righteousness, arise,
    Triumph o'er the Shades of Night:
Day-spring from on high, be near:
Day-star, in my Heart appear.

Dark and chearless is the Morn
　　Unaccompanied by Thee,
Joyless is the Day's Return,
　　'Till thy Mercy's Beams I see;
'Till they inward Light impart,
Glad my Eyes, and warm my Heart.

Visit then this Soul of mine,
　　Pierce the Gloom of Sin and Grief,
Fill me, Radiancy Divine,
　　Scatter all my Unbelief,
More and more Thyself display,
Shining to the perfect Day.

WAITING FOR CHRIST

Unchangeable, Almighty LORD,
　　The true, and merciful, and just,
Be mindful of thy gracious Word,
　　Wherein Thou causest me to trust.

My weary Eyes look out in vain,
　　And long thy saving Health to see:
But known to Thee is all my Pain,
　　When wilt Thou come, and comfort me.

Prisoner of Hope, to Thee I turn,
　　Thee my strong Hold, and only Stay:
Harden'd in Grief, I ever mourn:
　　Why do thy Chariot-wheels delay?

But shall thy Creature ask Thee why?
　　No; I retract the eager Prayer:
LORD, as Thou wilt, and not as I;
　　I cannot chuse: Thou canst not err.

To Thee, the only wise and true,
    See then at last I all resign;
Make me in CHRIST a Creature new,
    The Manner and the Time be Thine.

Only preserve my Soul from Sin,
    Nor let me faint for Want of Thee:
I'll wait 'till Thou appear *within*,
    And plant thy Heaven of Love in me.

IN TEMPTATION

JESU, Lover of my Soul,
    Let me to thy Bosom fly,
While the nearer Waters roll,
    While the Tempest still is high:
Hide me, O my Saviour, hide,
    'Till the Storm of Life is past:
Safe into the Haven guide;
    O receive my Soul at last.

Other Refuge have I none,
    Hangs my helpless Soul on Thee:
Leave, ah! leave me not alone,
    Still support and comfort me.
All my Trust on Thee is stay'd;
    All my Help from Thee I bring;
Cover my defenceless Head
    With the Shadow of thy Wing.

Wilt Thou not regard my Call?
    Wilt Thou not accept my Prayer?
Lo! I sink, I faint, I fall—
    Lo! on Thee I cast my Care:
Reach me out thy gracious Hand!
    While I of thy Strength receive,
Hoping against Hope I stand,
    Dying, and behold I live!

Thou, O CHRIST, art all I want,
 More than all in Thee I find:
Raise the Fallen, chear the Faint,
 Heal the Sick, and lead the Blind.
Just, and holy is thy Name,
 I am all Unrighteousness,
False, and full of Sin I am,
 Thou art full of Truth and Grace.

Plenteous Grace with Thee is found,
 Grace to cover all my Sin;
Let the healing Streams abound,
 Make, and keep me pure within:
Thou of Life the Fountain art:
 Freely let me take of Thee,
Spring Thou up within my Heart,
 Rise to all Eternity.

WRITTEN IN STRESS OF TEMPTATION

I am the Man who long have known
 The Fierceness of Temptation's Rage!
And still to GOD for Help I groan:
 When shall my Groans his Help engage?

Out of the Deep on CHRIST I call,
 In Bitterness of Spirit cry;
Broken upon that Stone I fall;
 I fall; the chief of Sinners I!

Saviour of Men, my sad Complaint
 Let me into thy Bosom pour:
Beneath my Load of Sin I faint,
 And Hell is ready to devour.

A Devil to myself I am,
 Yet cannot 'scape the Flesh I tear,
Beast, Fiend, and Legion is my Name,
 My Lot the Blackness of Despair.

Why then in this unequal Strife,
 To *Tophet's* utmost Margin driven,
Still gasps my parting Soul for Life,
 Nor quite gives up her Claim to Heaven?

Why hopes for Help my drooping Heart,
 (Hopes against Hope) when none is nigh
I cannot from my LORD depart,
 But kiss the Feet at which I die.

My LORD, (I still will call Thee mine,
 'Till sentenc'd to eternal Pain;)
Thou wouldest not thy Cup decline,
 The Vengeance due to guilty Man.

My Sufferings all to Thee are known,
 Tempted in every Point like me:
Regard my Griefs, regard thine own:
 JESU, remember Calvary!

O call to mind thine earnest Prayers,
 Thine Agony, and Sweat of Blood,
Thy strong and bitter Cries and Tears,
 Thy mortal Groan, *My* GOD, *my* GOD!

For whom didst Thou the Cross endure?
 Who nail'd thy Body to the Tree?
Did not thy Death my Life procure?
 O let thy Bowels answer me!

Art Thou not touch'd with human Woe?
 Hath Pity left the Son of Man?
Dost Thou not all our Sorrow know,
 And claim a Share in all our Pain?

Canst Thou forget thy Days of Flesh?
    Canst Thou *my* Miseries not feel?
Thy tender Heart it bleeds afresh:
    It bleeds; and Thou art JESUS still!

I feel, I feel Thee now the same,
    Kindled thy kind Relentings are;
These Meltings from thy Bowels came,
    Thy Spirit groan'd this inward Prayer.

Thy Prayer is heard, thy Will is done!
    Light in thy Light at length I see;
Thou wilt preserve my Soul thine own,
    And shew forth all thy Power in me.

My Peace returns, my Fears retire,
    I find Thee lifting up my Head,
Trembling I now to Heaven aspire,
    And hear the Voice that wakes the Dead.

Have I not heard, have I not known,
    That Thou the Everlasting LORD,
Whom Earth and Heaven their Maker own,
    Art always faithful to thy Word?

Thou wilt not break a bruised Reed,
    Or quench the faintest Spark of Grace,
'Till thro' the Soul thy Power is spread,
    Thine all-victorious Righteousness.

With Labour faint Thou wilt not fail,
    Or wearied give the Sinner o'er,
'Till in this Earth thy Judgment dwell,
    And born of GOD I sin no more.

The Day of small and feeble Things
    I know Thou never wilt despise;
I know, with Healing in his Wings,
    The Sun of Righteousness shall rise

My Heart Thou wilt anew create,
    The Fulness of thy Spirit give:
In stedfast Hope for this I wait,
    And confident in CHRIST believe.

FOR THE ANNIVERSARY DAY OF ONE'S CONVERSION

Glory to GOD, and Praise, and Love,
    Be ever, ever given;
By Saints below, and Saints above,
    The Church in Earth and Heaven.

On this glad Day the glorious Sun
    Of Righteousness arose,
On my benighted Soul He shone,
    And fill'd it with Repose.

Sudden expir'd the legal Strife,
    'Twas then I ceas'd to grieve,
My second, real, living Life,
    I then began to live.

Then with my *Heart* I first believ'd,
    Believ'd with Faith divine,
Power with the Holy Ghost receiv'd,
    To call the Saviour *mine*.

I felt my LORD's atoning Blood
    Close to *my* Soul applied;
Me, me He lov'd—the Son of GOD
    For *me*, for *me* He died!

I found, and own'd his Promise true,
    Ascertain'd of *my* Part,
My Pardon pass'd in Heaven I *knew*,
    When written on my Heart.

O for a thousand Tongues to sing
  My dear Redeemer's Praise!
The Glories of my GOD and King,
  The Triumphs of his Grace.

My gracious Master, and my GOD,
  Assist me to proclaim,
To spread thro' all the Earth abroad
  The Honours of thy Name.

JESUS the Name that charms our Fears,
  That bids our Sorrows cease;
'Tis Music in the Sinner's Ears,
  'Tis Life, and Health, and Peace!

He breaks the Power of cancell'd Sin,
  He sets the Prisoner free:
His Blood can make the Foulest clean,
  His Blood avail'd for *me*.

He speaks; and listening to his Voice,
  New Life the Dead receive,
The mournful, broken Hearts rejoice,
  The humble Poor *believe*.

Hear Him, ye Deaf; his Praise, ye Dumb,
  Your loosen'd Tongues employ;
Ye Blind, behold your Saviour come;
  And leap, ye Lame, for Joy.

Look unto Him, ye Nations; own
  Your GOD; ye fallen Race!
Look and be sav'd thro' Faith alone;
  Be justified by Grace.

See all your Sins on JESUS laid;
  The Lamb of GOD was slain,
His Soul was once an Offering made
  For *every Soul* of Man.

Harlots, and Publicans, and Thieves,
    In holy Triumph join!
Sav'd is the Sinner that believes,
    From Crimes as great as mine.

Murderers, and all ye hellish Crew,
    Ye Sons of Lust and Pride,
Believe the Saviour died for you;
    For me the Saviour died.

Awake from guilty Nature's Sleep,
    And CHRIST shall give you Light:
Call all your Sins into the Deep,
    And wash the *Ethiop* white.

With me, your Chief you then shall *know*,
    Shall feel your Sins forgiven;
Anticipate your Heaven below,
    And own that Love is Heaven.

Hymns and Sacred Poems, 1739 and 1740 (From the 5th Edition, 1756)

Make me a Clean Heart, O GOD, and renew a right Spirit within me.

Psalm ii. 10

O For an Heart to praise my GOD,
    An Heart from Sin set free!
An Heart that always feels Thy Blood,
    So freely spilt for Me!

An Heart resign'd, submissive, meek,
    My dear Redeemer's Throne,
Where only CHRIST is heard to speak,
    Where JESUS reigns alone.

An humble, lowly, contrite Heart,
    Believing, true, and clean,
Which neither Life nor Death can part
    From him that dwells within.

An Heart in Every Thought renew'd,
    And full of Love Divine,
Perfect, and right, and pure and good,
    A Copy, LORD, of Thine.

Thy tender Heart is still the same,
    And melts at Human Woe:
JESU, for Thee distrest I am,
    I want Thy Love to know.

My Heart, Thou know'st can never rest,
    Till Thou create my Peace,
Till of my Eden repossest,
    From Self, and Sin I cease.

Fruit of Thy gracious Lips, on Me
    Bestow that Peace unknown,
The Hidden Manna, and the Tree
    Of Life, and the White Stone.

Thy Nature, dearest LORD, impart,
    Come quickly from above,
Write Thy New Name upon my Heart,
    Thy New, Best Name of Love.

WRESTLING JACOB

Come, O Thou Traveller unknown,
    Whom still I hold, but cannot see,
My Company before is gone,
    And I am left alone with Thee,
With Thee all Night I mean to stay,
And wrestle till the Break of Day.

    I need not tell Thee who I am,
      My Misery, or Sin declare,
Thyself hast call'd me by my Name,
      Look on Thy Hands, and read it there,
But who, I ask Thee, who art Thou,
Tell me Thy Name, and tell me now?

    In vain Thou strugglest to get free,
      I never will unloose my Hold:
Art Thou the Man that died for me?
      The Secret of Thy Love unfold;
Wrestling I will not let Thee go,
Till I Thy Name, Thy Nature know.

    Wilt Thou not yet to me reveal
      Thy new, unutterable Name?
Tell me, I still beseech Thee, tell,
      To know it Now resolv'd I am;
Wrestling I will not let Thee go,
Till I Thy Name, Thy Nature know.

    'Tis all in vain to hold Thy Tongue,
      Or touch the Hollow of my Thigh:
Though every Sinew be unstrung,
      Out of my Arms Thou shalt not fly;
Wrestling I will not let Thee go,
Till I Thy Name, Thy Nature know.

    What tho' my shrinking Flesh complain,
      And murmur to contend so long,
I rise superior to my Pain,
      When I am weak then I am strong,
And when my All of Strength shall fail,
I shall with the GOD-man prevail.

My Strength is gone, my Nature dies,
   I sink beneath Thy weighty Hand,
Faint to revive, and fall to rise;
   I fall, and yet by Faith I stand,
I stand, and will not let Thee go,
Till I Thy Name, Thy Nature know.

Yield to me Now—for I am weak;
   But confident in Self-despair:
Speak to my Heart, in Blessings speak,
   Be conquer'd by my Instant Prayer,
Speak, or Thou never hence shalt move,
And tell me, if Thy Name is LOVE.

'Tis Love, 'tis Love! Thou diedst for Me,
   I hear Thy Whisper in my Heart.
The Morning breaks, the Shadows flee:
   Pure UNIVERSAL LOVE Thou art,
To me, to All Thy Bowels move,
Thy Nature, and Thy Name is LOVE.

My Prayer hath Power with GOD; the Grace
   Unspeakable I now receive,
Thro' Faith I see Thee Face to Face,
   I see Thee Face to Face, and live:
In vain I have not wept, and strove,
Thy Nature, and Thy Name is LOVE.

I know Thee, Saviour, who Thou art,
   JESUS the feeble Sinner's Friend;
Nor wilt Thou with the Night depart,
   But stay, and love me to the End;
Thy Mercies never shall remove,
Thy Nature, and Thy Name is LOVE.

The Sun of Righteousness on Me
    Hath rose with Healing in his Wings,
Wither'd my Nature's Strength; from Thee
    My Soul it's Life and Succour brings,
My Help is all laid up above;
Thy Nature, and Thy Name is LOVE.

    Contented now upon my Thigh
      I halt, till Life's short Journey end;
All Helplesness, all Weakness I,
    On Thee alone for Strength depend,
Nor have I Power, from Thee, to move;
Thy Nature, and Thy Name is LOVE.

    Lame as I am, I take the Prey,
      Hell, Earth, and Sin with Ease o'ercome;
I leap for Joy, pursue my Way,
    And as a bounding Hart fly home,
Thro' all Eternity to prove
Thy Nature, and Thy Name is LOVE.

HYMN FOR CHILDREN

GENTLE JESUS, meek, and mild,
Look upon a Little Child,
Pity my Simplicity,
Suffer me to come to Thee.

Fain I would to Thee be brought,
Dearest GOD, forbid it not,
Give me, dearest GOD, a Place
In the Kingdom of Thy Grace.

Put Thy Hands upon my Head,
Let me in Thine Arms be stayed,
Let me lean upon Thy Breast,
Lull me, lull me, LORD, to Rest.

Hold me fast in Thy Embrace,
Let me see Thy smiling Face,
Give me, LORD, Thy Blessing give,
Pray for me, and I shall live.

I shall live the Simple Life,
Free from Sin's uneasy Strife,
Sweetly ignorant of Ill,
Innocent, and happy still.

O that I may never know
What the Wicked People do;
Sin is contrary to Thee,
Sin is the Forbidden Tree.

Keep me from the great Offence,
Guard my helpless Innocence;
Hide me, from all Evil hide,
Self, and Stubborness, and Pride.

Lamb of GOD, I look to Thee,
Thou shalt my Example be;
Thou art gentle, meek, and mild,
Thou wast once a Little Child.

Fain I would be, as Thou art,
Give me thy obedient Heart;
Thou art pitiful and kind,
Let me have Thy loving Mind.

Meek, and lowly may I be,
Thou art all Humility;
Let me to my Betters bow,
Subject to Thy Parents Thou.

Let me above all fulfil
GOD my Heavenly Father's Will,
Never His Good Spirit grieve,
Only to His Glory live.

Thou didst live to GOD alone,
Thou didst never seek Thine own;
Thou Thyself didst never please,
GOD was all Thy Happiness.

Loving JESU, gentle Lamb,
In Thy gracious Hands I am,
Make me, Saviour, what Thou art,
Live Thyself within my Heart.

I shall then shew forth Thy Praise,
Serve Thee all my happy Days;
Then the World shall always see
CHRIST, the Holy Child, in Me.

Hymns and Sacred Poems, 1742

Some put their Trust in Chariots,
And Horses some rely on,
But GOD alone
Our Help we own,
GOD is the Strength of Sion.

His Name we will remember
In every sore Temptation,
And feel its Powers,
For CHRIST is ours,
With all his great Salvation.

We are his ransom'd People,
And He that bought will have us,
Secure from Harm,
Whilst JESUS' Arm
Is still stretch'd out to save us.

He out of all our Troubles
Shall mightily deliver,
    And then receive
    Us up, to live
And reign with him for ever.

Hymns for Times of Trouble [1745?]

FOR ONE IN PAIN

Pain, my old Companion Pain,
    Seldom parted from my Side,
Welcome to thy Seat again,
    Here, if GOD permits, abide:
Pledge of sure-approaching Ease,
    Haste to stop my wretched Breath,
Rugged Messenger of Peace,
    Joyful Harbinger of Death.

Foe to Nature as thou art,
    I embrace thee as my Friend:
Thou shalt bid my Griefs depart,
    Bring me to my Journey's End:
Yes, I joyfully decay,
    Homeward thro' thy Help I haste;
Thou hast shook the House of Clay;
    Surely it will fall at last.

Kind Remembrancer, To Thee
    Many a chearful Thought I owe:
Witness of Mortality,
    Wise thro' Thee my End I know;
Warn'd by every Pain I feel
    Of my Dissolution near;
Pleas'd the lessening Hours I tell:
    Quickly shall the Last be here.

Sacred, salutary Ill,
    Thee though foolish Man miscall,
Mingled by my Father's Skill;
    Sweet as Honey is the Gall:
Who beneath thy Pressure groan,
    Chief of Ills who reckon Thee,
Sin alas! they ne'er have known:
    Sin is perfect Misery.

Free from Sin I soon shall live,
    Free from Sin while here below,
Only thou mayst still survive,
    'Till the Joys of Heaven I know,
Of my Starry Crown possest;
    All thy Office then is o'er,
When I gain the Glorious Rest,
    Pain and Suffering are no more.

AFTER PREACHING TO THE NEWCASTLE COLLIERS

Who are These that come from far,
    Swifter than a flying Cloud!
Thick as flocking Doves they are,
    Eager in pursuit of GOD:
Trembling as the Storm draws nigh,
    Hastning to their Place of Rest,
See them to the Windows fly,
    To the Ark of JESU'S Breast!

Who are These but Sinners poor,
    Conscious of their lost Estate,
Sin-sick Souls, who for their Cure
    On the good Physician wait;
Fallen who bewail their Fall,
    Proffer'd Mercy who embrace,
Listning to the Gospel-Call,
    Longing to be saved by Grace.

135

For his Mate the Turtle moans,
    For his GOD the Sinner sighs;
Hark, the Music of their Groans,
    Humble Groans that pierce the Skies!
Surely GOD their Sorrows hears,
    Every Accent, every Look,
Treasures up their gracious Tears,
    Notes their Sufferings in his Book.

He who hath their Cure begun,
    Will He now despise their Pain?
Can He leave his Work undone,
    Bring them to the Birth in vain?
No; we all who seek shall find,
    We who ask shall all receive,
Be to CHRIST in Spirit join'd,
    Free from Sin forever live.

Hymns and Sacred Poems, 1749

ON THE SIGHT OF A CORPSE

Ah lovely Appearance of Death!
    No Sight upon Earth is so fair;
Not all the gay Pageants that *breathe*
    Can with a dead Body compare:
With solemn Delight I survey
    The Corpse when the Spirit is fled,
In love with the beautiful Clay,
    And longing to lie in its stead.

How blest is our Brother, bereft
    Of all that could burthen his Mind,
How easy the Soul that hath left
    This wearisome Body behind!

Of Evil incapable Thou,
    Whose Relicks with Envy I see,
No longer in Misery now,
    No longer a Sinner like me.

This Earth is affected no more
    With Sickness, or shaken with Pain,
The War in the Members is o'er,
    And never shall vex him again:
No Anger henceforward, or Shame,
    Shall redden this innocent Clay,
Extinct is the animal Flame,
    And Passion is vanish'd away.

The languishing Head is at rest,
    Its Thinking and Aching are o'er,
The quiet immoveable Breast
    Is heav'd by Affliction no more:
The Heart is no longer the Seat
    Of Trouble and torturing Pain,
It ceases to flutter and beat,
    It never shall flutter again.

The Lids He so seldom could close,
    By Sorrow forbidden to sleep,
Seal'd up in eternal Repose,
    Have strangely forgotten to weep:
The Fountains can yield no Supplies,
    These Hollows from Water are free,
The Tears are all wip'd from these Eyes,
    And Evil they never shall see.

To mourn, and to suffer, is mine,
    While bound in a Prison I breathe,
And still for Deliverance pine,
    And press to the Issues of Death:

What now with my Tears I bedew,
    O might I this Moment become,
My Spirit created a-new,
    My Flesh be consign'd to the Tomb.

Funeral Hymns, 3rd edition, 1753

THY KINGDOM COME!

Lo! He comes with clouds discending,
    Once for favour'd sinners slain!
Thousand, thousand saints attending,
    Swell the triumph of his train:
        Hallelujah,
    GOD appears, on earth to reign!

Every eye shall now behold Him
    Rob'd in dreadful majesty,
Those who set at nought and sold Him,
    Pierc'd, and nail'd Him to the tree,
        Deeply wailing
    Shall the true Messiah see.

The dear tokens of his passion
    Still his dazling body bears,
Cause of endless exultation
    To his ransom'd worshippers;
        With what rapture
    Gaze we on those glorious scars!

Yea, amen! let all adore Thee
    High on thine eternal throne
Saviour, take the power and glory
    Claim the kingdom for thine own:
        JAH, JEHOVAH,
    Everlasting GOD, come down.

Hymns of Intercession for All Mankind, 1758

ON THE DEATH OF A CHILD

Dead! dead! the Child I lov'd so well!
Transported to the world above!
I need no more my heart conceal:
I never dar'd indulge my love:
But may I not indulge my grief,
And seek in tears a sad relief?

Mine earthly happiness is fled,
His mother's joy, his father's hope,
(O had I dy'd in *Isaac's* stead!)
He *should* have liv'd, my age's prop,
He should have clos'd his father's eyes,
And follow'd me to paradise.

But hath not heaven, who first bestow'd,
A right to take his gifts away?
I bow me to the sovereign GOD,
Who snatch'd him from the evil day!
Yet nature *will* repeat her moan,
And fondly cry, "My son, my son!"

Turn from him, turn, officious thought!
Officious thought presents again
The thousand little acts he wrought,
Which wound my heart with soothing pain:
His looks, his winning gestures rise,
His waving hands, and laughing eyes!

Those waving hands no more shall move,
Those laughing eyes shall smile no more:
He cannot now engage our love,
With sweet insinuating power
Our weak unguarded hearts insnare,
And rival his Creator there.

139

From us, as we from him, secure,
    Caught to his heavenly Father's breast,
He waits, till we the bliss insure,
    From all these stormy sorrows rest,
And see him with our Angel stand,
To waft, and welcome us to land.

          Funeral Hymns, 2nd series, 1759

FOR A CHILD CUTTING HIS TEETH

Suffering for another's sin,
    Why should innocence complain?
Sin by Adam enter'd in,
    Sin ingendring grief and pain:
Sin entail'd on all our race,
    Forces harmless babes to cry,
Born to sorrow and distress,
    Born to feel, lament, and die.

Tortur'd in his tender frame,
    Strugling with convulsive throes,
Doth he not aloud proclaim
    Guilt the cause of all our woes?
Guilt, whose sad effects appear,
    Guilt original we own,
See it in that starting tear,
    Hear it in that heaving groan!

Man's intemperate offence
    In its punishment we read;
Speechless, by his aching sense
    Guilty doth our infant plead;
Instruments of sin and pain,
    Signs of guilt and misery
Eve's incontinence explain,
    Point us to the Tasted Tree.

There the bitter root we find,
    Fatal source of nature's ill,
Ill which all our fallen kind
    With this young apostate feel:
But what we can ne'er remove
    Jesus came to sanctify,
Second Adam from above
    Born for us to live and die.

Help, the woman's heavenly Seed,
    Thou that didst our sorrows take,
Turn aside the death decreed,
    Save him for thy nature's sake!
Pitying Son of man and God,
    Still thy creature's pains indure;
Quench the fever with thy blood,
    Bless him with a perfect cure.

Thine it is to bless and heal,
    Thine to rescue and repair:
On our child the answer seal,
    Thou who didst suggest the prayer:
Send salvation to this house;
    Then to double health restor'd,
I, and mine will pay our vows,
    I and mine will serve the Lord.

THE COLLIER'S HYMN

Teacher, Friend of foolish sinners,
        Take the praise of thy grace
    From us young beginners.
Struck with loving admiration
        Hear us tell Of thy zeal
    For our soul's salvation.

Foes to God and unforgiven
  Once we were, Distant far,
 Far as hell from heaven:
But we have thro' Thee found favour,
  Brought to God By thy blood,
 O Thou precious Saviour.

Thou hast in the weak and feeble
  Power display'd, Call'd and made
 Us thy favourite people:
Us the vulgar, and obscure
  Thou dost own; Us unknown,
 Ignorant and poor.

Simple folk and undiscerning,
  Nothing we Know but Thee,
 Love is all our learning:
We with loving hearts adore thee,
  This our deep Scholarship,
 This is all our glory.

Thou, we know, hast died to save us,
  We are thine, Love Divine,
 Thou who bought'st shalt have us:
Taught and led by thy good Spirit
  We shall soon Share thy throne,
 All thy joys inherit.

Here is knowledge rare, and hidden
  From the wise, Who despise
 All our inward Eden:
Thou to us the truth hast given,
  We in Thee, (Happy we!)
 Know the way to heaven.

THE YOUNG MAN'S HYMN

How shall a young unstable man
    To evil prone like me,
His actions and his heart maintain
    From all pollution free?
Thee, Lord, that I may not forsake,
    Or ever turn aside,
Thy precepts for my rule I take,
    Thy Spirit for my Guide.

Govern'd by the ingrafted word,
    And principled with grace,
I shall not yield to sin abhor'd,
    Or give to passion place:
From youthful lusts I still shall flee,
    From all the paths of vice,
My omnipresent Saviour see,
    And walk before thine eyes.

Saviour, to me thy Spirit give,
    That thro' his power I may
Thy word effectually believe,
    And faithfully obey;
From every great transgression pure,
    For all thy will prepar'd,
Thy servant to the end endure,
    And gain the full reward.

Hymns for the use of Families, 1767

JUST BEFORE THEIR BEING LED OUT TO EXECUTION

Justice, thy summons we obey,
And come our forfeit lives to pay,
While God and man we justify,
And by a righteous sentence die!

But the great God in whom we trust
Is merciful, as well as just:
And Jesu's blood for sin atones,
And will not let us die but once!

Jesus into thy hands we fall,
With our last breath for mercy call,
To thee our ransom'd spirits commend,
And hope, that heaven is in our end.

Because thou hangedst on a tree,
And didst thyself expire for me,
Me and my dying mates receive,
And bid our souls for ever live!

Prayers for Condemned Malefactors, 1785

WRITTEN ON THE DAY OF HIS [DR. DODD'S]
EXECUTION, JUNE 27, 1777

Refuge supreme of sad despair,
    The outcast's Hope, the sinner's Friend,
For him we breathe our latest prayer,
    Whose life hath reach'd its shameful end:
For him we in Thy Spirit groan,
And bear our burden to the throne.

The mercy which he sought from man,
    From cruel man he could not find;
But can he ask Thy grace in vain?
    Lover and Saviour of mankind,
Thy mercy and *Thy* grace impart,
And fill with peace his happy heart.

Give him the sting of death to feel,
    With all his cancell'd sins removed;

Now in his soul Thyself reveal,
    So dearly bought, so dearly loved;
Challenge his parting soul for Thine,
And swallow' up death in life Divine!

from Ms sources

Robert Seagrave. 1693–1760?

DRAWING

Wash and be clean, the Spirit cries;
In our own Streams, vain man replies;
    These too my Soul avow'd;
Hence I at broken Cisterns stay'd,
And ev'ry feeble Art essay'd,
    A Sinner poor and proud!

Jordan was nam'd, not I would move,
But for *Damascus'* Rivers strove,
    Nor other would I crave;
Bethesda's Pool made many clean;
But none was near to put me in,
    To try the troubled Wave.

Immanuel my Mis'ry saw,
Knew how to cure, and how to draw,
    With Cords of Love he stood;
He drew me to the joyful Sound,
And by it on my parched Ground
    Pour'd the refreshing Flood.

The News of his all-healing Blood,
For helpless Sinners, oh how good!
    This ev'ry pain removes:
How free the purple Fountain flows,
How deep the healing Balsam goes,
    Each glad Believer proves!

145

And now all other Streams I leave,
And to the bleeding Saviour cleave,
   Safe only in his side;
No other scheme shall me employ,
At this one Spring of Peace and Joy
   Ever let me abide.

THE PILGRIM'S SONG

Rise my Soul, and stretch thy Wings,
   Thy better Portion trace;
Rise from transitory Things,
   Tow'rds Heav'n thy native Place.
Sun and Moon, and Stars decay,
   Time shall soon this Earth remove;
Rise, my Soul, and haste away
   To Seats prepar'd above.

Rivers to the Ocean run,
   Nor stay in all their Course;
Fire ascending seeks the Sun,
   Both speed them to their Source.
So my Soul deriv'd from God,
   Pants to view his glorious Face;
Forward tends to his Abode,
   To rest in his Embrace.

Fly me Riches, fly me Cares,
   Whilst I that Coast explore;
Flatt'ring World, with all thy snares,
   Solicit me no more.
Pilgrims fix not here their Home;
   Strangers tarry but a Night,
When the last dear Morn is come,
   They'll rise to joyful Light.

Cease, ye Pilgrims, cease to mourn,
    Press onward to the Prize;
Soon our Saviour will return
    Triumphant in the Skies.
Yet a Season and you know
    Happy Entrance will be giv'n,
All our Sorrows left below,
    And Earth exchang'd for Heav'n.

Hymns for Christian Worship, 1742–1748; from D. Sedgwick's reprint, 1860

William Hammond. 1719–1783

I knew that thou wouldst deal very treacherously.

Isa. xlviii. 8

How gracious is the LORD,
    To such a Wretch as me,
Who trample on his Word,
    And from his Precepts flee;
His Precepts, which I can't but own,
Are Good and easy to be done!

A Cage of Birds unclean,
    My Heart inclines to Ill,
I am in Love with Sin,
    And near allied to Hell:
LORD, wilt thou shew thy Mercy Free,
In saving Vile Apostate me?

Beside myself I am,
    I know not what I do;
A Sinner is my Name,
    Damnation is my Due:
JESU, wilt Thou the Curse remove,
And send Remission from above?

What mortal Tongue can tell
    The Depths of Sin in me?
As wide and deep as Hell
    Is my Iniquity;
Yet, LORD, am I beyond the Line
Of Love unsearchable like Thine?

I groan to be set free
    From Sin's impure Remains;
I cry for Liberty,
        LORD, break my Iron Chains:
JESU, when shall I in me find
The Transcript of thy Sinless Mind?

THE PREACHER IN A STRAIT

From Phil. i. 23, 24

Death is a Cure for ev'ry Ill,
    A Balm for ev'ry Wound:
How Safe, how Undisturb'd, how Still
    Men rest beneath the Ground!

When shall I lay my weary Head
    In Silence in the Grave,
And sleep secure among the Dead,
    And no more Sorrows have?

Oh! What a Pleasure 'tis to die!
    How Sweet to yield our Breath!
Life is a Mortal Malady,
    Whose only Cure is Death.

Yet make me Willing, LORD, to stay
    Till Thou dost call me hence,
Then chearfully thy Voice obey,
    And put off Flesh and Sense.

Gladly would I prolong my Days,
    To feed thy Flock, O GOD,
Which Thou hast justified by Grace,
    And purchas'd with thy Blood.

How am I straitned betwixt Two!
    I know not which to choose:
Dear Saviour, teach me which to do,
    Teach me which to refuse.

        Psalms, Hymns and Spiritual Songs, 1745

William Williams. 1717–1791

The End of all Things is at Hand

1 Pet, iv. 7

The Moon and all her Train surrounding
    With the lofty dazzling Sun,
Now are wearied in the Heavens
    Their laborious Course to run.
Earth and Sea in mighty Travail
    With their Creatures never cease,
Groaning for the Revelation,
    Glorious of the Sons of Peace.

Ev'ry Hour doth call, "Be Ready,
    Haste to *Zoar*, there to remain;
Fire and Brimstone hover over
    All the Cities of the Plain."
Snatch me from the Conflagration,
    Jesus, draw me by the Hand,
Lest I love my antient Dwelling,
    And transgress thy great Command.

149

Death is fond in Expectation,
    Creeping forward unaware;
All my frail and feeble Members
    Under his Dominion are;
Every Artery and Muscle
    His approaching Conquest beat,
Here he aims a Blow decisive
    Which he never needs repeat.

Strike, O Death, but first consider
    Who is He that's on my Side;
Alpha, Omega, the Creator,
    Cloath'd in human Flesh and dy'd;
Whilst thou level'st at my Structure,
    To his bleeding Wounds I'll flee;
I shall live and be exalted
    When Confusion shatters thee.

Yet my foes are bold and daring,
    And are many, I but one,
But the mighty glorious Jesus
    Conquest over all hath won.
Fear is banish'd, Death is nothing,
    And the Grave an easy Bed
To Believers, since our Nature
    To the Godhead hath been wed.

Sing, my Soul, at the approaching
    From the Prison to Depart,
Where abundance of Distempers
    Death hath sow'd in every Part.
Soul, mount to thy holy Mansion,
    Body, slumber in the Ground;
In the Morning every Atom
    Of thy Ashes will be found.

Hosannah to the Son of David, 1759; from D. Sedgwick's reprint,
1859

HYMN

Lord, when I make my Passage thro'
Great Jordan, that doth overflow
    Its Banks eternal, deep and wide,
Stretch forth thy Hand without Delay,
Give not my Soul to Death a Prey—
    In deepest Stream stand by my Side.

There by my Side when Thee I have,
I do not fear the strongest Wave;
    Tho' I am weak, great is thy Might:
Thy Strength can hold me on my Way,
When thousand Perils do dismay,
    And thousand Enemies affright.

Blessed are all that trust in Thee,
And thy Salvation long to see;
    Thy Promises thou wilt fulfil:
Our Souls shall taste those streams of Love,
That issues from the Throne above;
    The Fruits of thy eternal Will.

HYMN

    I am daunted all the Day
        By innumerable Foes,
    My Enemy in Strength
        And Arrogancy grows;
O Man divine! pour down thy Grace,
They all dissolve before thy Face.

    I groan under the Weight
        Of Burdens vast, unknown;
    I'll faint away, and die,
        If here left alone;
My days are spent, O Saviour, speed!
And help a Wretch in Time of Need.

O let me hear that Voice
That sets the Captive free;
And give a true Release
From wretched Misery;
That my Delight may be to adore,
And praise thy Name for evermore.

Gloria in Excelsis, 1772; from D. Sedgwick's reprint, 1859

A FAVOURITE HYMN

Guide me, O Thou great Jehovah,
Pilgrim through this barren land;
I am weak, but Thou are Mighty,
Hold me with Thy pow'rful hand
Bread of heaven, bread of heaven!
Feed me till I want no more.

Open now the chrystal fountain,
Whence the healing stream doth flow;
Let the fire and cloudy pillar
Lead me all my journey thro':
Strong deliv'rer, Strong deliv'rer,
Be Thou still my *Strength* and *Shield*.

When I tread the verge of Jordan,
Bid my anxious fears subside;
Death of death's, and hell's destruction,
Land me safe on Canaan's side:
Songs of praises, songs of praises,
I will ever give to thee.

Musing on my habitation,
Musing on my heav'nly home,
Fills my soul with holy longing,
Come, my Jesus, quickly come;
Vanity is all I see,
Lord, I long to be with Thee!

A leaflet, 1772

Augustus Montague Toplady. 1740–1778

IN TEMPTATION

Compass'd by the Foe, on thee
 Feebly I presume to call;
Get thyself the Victory,
 Hold me and I shall not fall:
On thy Creature Mercy shew,
Thine I am by Purchase too.

Guard of my defenceless Heart,
 Wherefore hidest thou thy Face?
Mercy's Fountain Head thou art,
Ever full of Truth and Grace:
Quell the roaring Lion's pow'r;
Father, save me from this Hour!

Sun of Righteousness, arise,
 Shed thy blissful Rays on me;
Kindly listen to my Cries,
 Try'd by Him who tempted Thee:
Thou my helpless Soul defend,
Keep me blameless to the End.

Rise in Vengeance from thy Seat;
 JESUS, LORD, make haste to save:
Me, to sift my Soul as Wheat,
 Satan hath desir'd to have:
Let Him not too far prevail,
Suffer not my Faith to fail.

Try'd, afflicted and distrest
 By Temptation's searching Flame,
Tho', beneath its load opprest,
 Now in Heaviness I am,
I shall soon at Freedom be,
More than Conqueror in thee.

This Affliction shall work out,
    (Light and transient as it *is*)
When I am to *Sion* brought,
    Everlasting Joy and Peace:
Here but for a Moment try'd,
There for ever glorify'd.

        ★   ★   ★

Chain'd to the World, to Sin ty'd down,
    In Darkness still I lie;
Lord, break my Bonds, Lord, give me Wings,
    And teach me how to fly.

Instruct my feeble Hands to War,
    In me thy Strength reveal,
To put my ev'ry Lust to Death,
    And fight thy Battles well.

Rend ev'ry Veil that shades thy Face,
    Put on thine Helmet, Lord:
My Sin shall fall, my Guilt expire
    Beneath thy conqu'ring Sword.

Thou art the Mighty GOD of Hosts,
    Whose Counsels never fail;
Be thou my glorious Chief, and then
    I cannot but prevail.

Then slay my Sins without Reserve,
    Burn up each Lust in me;
Kill, kill my vain rebellious Heart,
    And I shall live to Thee.

Poems on Sacred Subjects, 1759; from D. Sedgwick's reprint, 1860

A CHAMBER HYMN

What tho' my frail Eyelids refuse
    Continual watching to keep,
And, punctual as Midnight renews,
    Demand the refreshment of Sleep;
A sov'reign Protector I have,
    Unseen, yet for ever at hand:
Unchangeably faithful to save,
    Almighty to rule and command.

From Evil secure, and its dread,
    I rest, if my Saviour is nigh;
And Songs his kind presence indeed
    Shall in the Night-season supply:
He smiles, and my Comforts abound;
    His grace as the Dew shall descend,
And Walls of Salvation surround
    The Soul He delights to defend.

Kind Author and Ground of my Hope,
    Thee, Thee for my God I avow;
My glad Ebenezer set up,
    And own Thou hast help'd me till now:
I muse on the Years that are past,
    Wherein my Defence thou hast prov'd;
Nor wilt thou relinquish, at last,
    A Sinner so signally lov'd.

Beneficent Hearer of Pray'r,
    Thou Feeder and Guardian of thine,
My All to thy covenant Care
    I, sleeping and waking, resign:
If thou art my Shield and my Sun,
    The Night is no darkness to me;
And, fast as my Moments roll on,
    They bring me but nearer to Thee.

Thy minist'ring Spirits descend,
 And watch while thy Saints are asleep;
By Day and Night they attend,
 The Heirs of Salvation to keep:
Bright Seraphs, dispatch'd from the Throne,
 Fly swift to their Stations assign'd;
And Angels elect are sent down
 To guard the elect of Mankind.

Thy Worship no interval knows:
 Their Fervour is still on the Wing;
And, while they protect my Repose,
 They Chant to the praise of my King:
I, too, at the Season ordain'd,
 Their Chorus for ever shall join;
And Love and Adore, without end,
 Their gracious Creator and mine.

Occasional Hymns 1760–1778; from Sedgwick, 1860

A LIVING AND DYING PRAYER FOR THE HOLIEST BELIEVER IN THE WORLD

Rock of Ages, cleft for me,
Let me hide myself in Thee!
Let the Water and the Blood,
From thy riven Side which flow'd,
Be of Sin the double Cure,
Cleanse me from its Guilt and Pow'r.

Not the labors of my hands
Can fullfill thy Law's demands:
Could my Zeal no respite know,
Could my tears forever flow,
All for Sin could not atone:
Thou must save, and Thou alone!

Nothing in my hand I bring;
Simply to thy Cross I cling;
Naked, come to Thee for Dress;
Helpless, look to Thee for grace;
Foul, I to the fountain fly:
Wash me, SAVIOR, or I die!

Whilst I draw this fleeting breath—
When my eye-strings break in death—
When I soar through tracts unknown—
See Thee on thy Judgement-Throne—
ROCK of ages, cleft for me,
Let me hide myself in THEE!

The Gospel Magazine, March, 1776

John Newton. 1725–1807

THE CREATURES IN THE LORD'S HANDS

The water stood like walls of brass,
To let the sons of Israel pass;
And from the rock in rivers burst,
At Moses' prayer to quench their thirst.

The fire restrain'd by GOD's commands,
Could only burn his people's bands;
Too faint, when he was with them there,
To singe their garments or their hair.

At Daniel's feet the lions lay
Like harmless lambs, nor touch'd their prey;
And ravens, which on carrion fed,
Procur'd Elijah flesh and bread.

Thus creatures only can fulfil
Their great Creator's holy will;
And when his servants need their aid,
His purposes must be obey'd.

So if his blessing he refuse,
Their pow'r to help they quickly lose,
Sure as on creatures we depend,
Our hopes in disappointment end.

Then let us trust the LORD alone,
And creature-confidence disown;
Nor if they threaten need we fear,
They cannot hurt if he be near.

If instruments of pain they prove,
Still are they guided by his love;
As lancets by the surgeon's skill,
Which wound to cure, and not to kill.

THE BENIGHTED TRAVELLER

Forest beasts, that live by prey,
Seldom shew themselves by day;
But when day-light is withdrawn,
Then they rove and roar till dawn.

Who can tell the traveller's fears,
When their horrid yells he hears?
Terror almost stops his breath,
While each step he looks for death.

Thus when JESUS is in view,
Cheerful I my way pursue;
Walking by my Saviour's light,
Nothing can my soul affright.

But when he forbears to shine,
Soon the travell'rs case is mine;
Lost, benighted, struck with dread,
What a painful path I tread!

Then, my soul with terror hears
Worse than lions, wolves, or bears,
Roaring loud in ev'ry part,
Thro' the forest of my heart.

Wrath, impatience, envy, pride,
Satan and his host beside,
Press around me to devour;
How can I escape their pow'r?

Gracious LORD afford me light,
Put these beasts of prey to flight;
Let thy pow'r and love be shewn,
Save me, for I am *thine* own.

THE BEE SAVED FROM THE SPIDER

The subtle spider often weaves
    His unsuspected snares,
Among the balmy flow'rs and leaves,
    To which the bee repairs.

When in his web he sees one hang,
    With a malicious joy,
He darts upon it with his fang,
    To poison and destroy.

How welcome then, some pitying friend,
    To save the threat'ned bee!
The spider's treach'rous web to rend,
    And set the captive free!

159

My soul has been in such a case,
    When first I knew the LORD,
I hasted to the means of grace,
    Where sweets I knew were stor'd.

Little I thought of danger near,
    That soon my joys would ebb;
But ah! I met a spider there,
    Who caught me in his web.

Then Satan rais'd his pois'nous sting,
    And aim'd his blows at me;
While I, poor helpless·trembling thing,
    Could neither fight nor flee.

But oh! the Saviour's pitying eye
    Reliev'd me from despair;
He saw me at the point to die
    And broke the fatal snare.

My case his heedless saints should warn,
    Or cheer them if afraid;
May you from me your danger learn,
    And where to look for aid.

ASK WHAT I SHALL GIVE THEE

Come, my soul, thy suit prepare,
JESUS loves to answer pray'r;
He himself has bid thee pray,
Therefore will not say thee nay.

Thou art coming to a King,
Large petitions with thee bring;
For his grace and pow'r are such,
None can ever ask too much.

With my burden I begin,
LORD, remove this load of sin!
Let thy blood, for sinners spilt,
Set my conscience free from guilt.

LORD! I come to thee for rest,
Take possession of my breast;
There thy blood-bought right maintain,
And without a rival reign.

As the image in the glass
Answers the beholder's face;
Thus unto my heart appear,
Print thine own resemblance there.

While I am a pilgrim here,
Let thy love my spirit cheer;
Be my Guide, my Guard, my Friend,
Lead me to my journey's end.

Shew me what I have to do,
Ev'ry hour my strength renew;
Let me live a life of faith,
Let me die thy people's death.

THE NAME OF JESUS

How sweet the name of JESUS sounds
    In a believer's ear?
It soothes his sorrows, heals his wounds,
    And drives away his fear.

It makes the wounded spirit whole,
    And calms the troubled breast;
'Tis Manna to the hungry soul,
    And to the weary rest.

Dear name! the rock on which I build,
    My shield and hiding place;
My never-failing treas'ry fill'd
    With boundless stores of grace.

By thee my pray'rs acceptance gain,
    Altho' with sin defil'd;
Satan accuses me in vain,
    And I am own'd a child.

JESUS! my Shepherd, Husband, Friend,
    My Prophet, Priest, and King;
My LORD, my Life, my Way, my End,
    Accept the praise I bring.

Weak is the effort of my heart,
    And cold my warmest thought;
But when I see thee as thou art,
    I'll praise thee as I ought.

'Till then I would thy love proclaim
    With every fleeting breath;
And may the music of thy name
    Refresh my soul in death.

ZION, OR THE CITY OF GOD

Glorious things of thee are spoken
Zion, city of our GOD!
He, whose word cannot be broken,
Form'd thee for his own abode:
On the rock of ages founded,
What can shake thy sure repose?
With salvation's walls surrounded,
Thou may'st smile at all thy foes.

See! the streams of living waters,
Springing from eternal love;
Well supply thy sons and daughters,
And all fear of want remove:
Who can faint while such a river
Ever flows their thirst t'assuage?
Grace, which like the LORD, the Giver,
Never fails from age to age.

Round each habitation hov'ring,
See the cloud and fire appear!
For a glory and a cov'ring,
Shewing that the LORD is near:
Thus deriving from their banner
Light by night and shade by day;
Safe they feed upon the Manna
Which he gives them when they pray.

Blest inhabitants of Zion,
Wash'd in the Redeemer's blood!
JESUS, whom their souls rely on,
Makes them kings and priests to GOD:
'Tis his love his people raises
Over self to reign as kings
And as priests, his solemn praises
Each for a thank-off'ring brings.

Saviour, if of Zion's city
I thro' grace a member am;
Let the world deride or pity,
I will glory in thy name:
Fading is the worldling's pleasure,
All his boasted pomp and show;
Solid joys and lasting treasure,
None but Zion's children know.

Olney Hymns, 1779

William Cowper. 1731–1800

Genesis v. 24

Oh! for a closer walk with GOD,
    A calm and heavenly frame;
A light to shine upon the road
    That leads me to the Lamb!

Where is the blessedness I knew
    When first I saw the LORD?
Where is the soul-refreshing view
    Of JESUS, and his word?

What peaceful hours I once enjoy'd!
    How sweet their mem'ry still!
But they have left an aching void,
    The world can never fill.

Return, O holy Dove, return,
    Sweet messenger of rest;
I hate the sins that made thee mourn,
    And drove thee from my breast.

The dearest idol I have known,
    Whate'er that idol be;
Help me to tear it from thy throne,
    And worship only thee.

So shall my walk be close with GOD,
    Calm and serene my frame;
So purer light shall mark the road
    That leads me to the Lamb.

PRAISE FOR THE FOUNTAIN OPENED

Zechariah xiii. 1

There is a fountain fill'd with blood,
  Drawn from EMMANUEL'S veins;
And sinners, plung'd beneath that flood,
  Loose all their guilty stains.

The dying thief rejoic'd to see
  That fountain in his day;
And there have I, as vile as he,
  Wash'd all my sins away.

Dear dying Lamb, thy precious blood,
  Shall never lose its pow'r;
Till all the ransom'd church of GOD
  Be sav'd, to sin no more.

E'er since, by faith, I saw the stream
  Thy flowing wounds supply:
Redeeming love has been my theme,
  And shall be till I die.

Then in a nobler sweeter song,
  I'll sing thy pow'r to save;
When this poor lisping stamm'ring tongue
  Lies silent in the grave.

LORD, I believe thou hast prepar'd,
  (Unworthy tho' I be)
For me a blood-bought free reward,
  A golden harp for me!

'Tis strung, and tun'd, for endless years,
  And form'd by power divine;
To sound, in GOD the Father's ears,
  No other name but thine.

LIGHT SHINING OUT OF DARKNESS

GOD moves in a mysterious way,
　His wonders to perform;
He plants his footsteps in the sea,
　And rides upon the storm.

Deep in unfathomable mines
　Of never-failing skill;
He treasures up his bright designs,
　And works his sovereign will.

Ye fearful saints fresh courage take,
　The clouds ye so much dread
Are big with mercy, and shall break
　In blessings on your head.

Judge not the LORD by feeble sense,
　But trust him for his grace;
Behind a frowning providence,
　He hides a smiling face.

His purposes will ripen fast,
　Unfolding ev'ry hour;
The bud may have a bitter taste,
　But sweet will be the flow'r.

Blind unbelief is sure to err,
　And scan his work in vain;
GOD is his own interpreter,
　And he will make it plain.

Olney Hymns, 1779

Hon. Walter Shirley. 1725–1786

GOOD FRIDAY

Flow fast my tears; the cause is great;
    This tribute claims an injur'd friend:
One whom I long pursu'd with hate,
    And yet He lov'd me to the end.
When death his terrors round me spread,
And aim'd his arrows at my head,
CHRIST interpos'd, the wound He bore,
And bade the monster dare no more.

Fast flow my tears, yet faster flow,
    Stream copious as yon purple tide,
'Twas I that dealt the deadly blow,
    I urg'd the hand that pierc'd his side,
Keen pangs and agonizing smart
Oppress his soul, and rend his heart;
While justice, arm'd with pow'r divine,
Pours on his head what's due to mine.

Fast and yet faster flow my tears,
    Love breaks the heart and drains the eyes;
His visage marr'd, tow'rds heav'n He rears,
    And, pleading for his murd'rer, dies!
My grief nor measure knows nor end,
Till He appears the sinner's friend;
And gives me in an happy hour,
To feel the risen SAVIOUR's pow'r.

INVITATION TO CHRIST

Sweet as the shepherd's tuneful reed
    From Sion's mount I heard the sound:
Gay sprang the flow'rets of the mead,
    And gladden'd nature smil'd around:
The voice of peace salutes mine ear;
CHRIST's lovely voice perfumes the air.

Peace, troubl'd soul, whose plaintive moan
    Hath taught these rocks the note of woe;
Cease thy complaint, suppress thy groan,
    And let thy tears forget to flow.
Behold, the precious balm is found,
Which lulls thy pain, which heals thy wound.

Come, freely come, by sin opprest,
    Unburthen here the weighty load;
Here find thy refuge, and thy rest,
    Safe on the bosom of thy GOD.
Thy GOD's thy SAVIOR, glorious word!
That sheaths th'avenger's glitt'ring sword.

As spring the winter, day the night,
    Peace sorrow's gloom shall chace away;
And smiling joy, a seraph bright,
    Shall tend thy steps and near Thee stay,
Whilst glory weaves th'immortal crown,
And waits to claim Thee for her own.

LOOKING UNTO CHRIST

Sweet the moments, rich in blessing,
    Which before the cross I spend;
Life and health, and peace possessing
    From the sinner's dying Friend.
Here I'll sit, for ever viewing
    Mercy's streams in streams of blood;
Precious drops my soul bedewing,
    Plead and claim my peace with GOD.

Truly blessed is this station,
    Low before his cross to lie;
While I see divine compassion
    Floating in his languid eye;

Here it is I find my heaven,
    While upon the LAMB I gaze;
Love I much? I've much forgiven,
    I'm a miracle of grace.

Love and grief my heart dividing,
    With my tears His feet I'll bathe:
Constant still in faith abiding,
    Life deriving from his death.
May I still enjoy this feeling,
    In all need to JESUS go;
Prove his wounds each day more healing,
    And Himself more deeply know!

*A Select Collection of Hymns ed. by the Countess of Huntingdon,
1780*

Anonymous

IMPUTED RIGHTEOUSNESS

Fair as the moon my robes appear,
    While graces are my dress:
Clear as the sun, while found to wear
    My SAVIOR's righteousness.

My moon-like graces, changing much,
    Are soil'd with many a spot:
My sun-like glory is not such;
    My SAVIOR changes not.

In Him array'd, my robes of light
    The morning rays outshine:
The stars of heav'n are not so bright,
    Nor angels half so fine.

Tho' hellish smoke my duties stain,
    And sin deform me quite;
The blood of JESUS makes me clean,
    And his obedience, white.

Then let the law in rigor stand,
  And for perfection call:
My LORD discharg'd the whole demand,
  My surety paid it all.

Let ev'ry high self-righteous thought
  Be utterly cast down:
Free-grace alone the work hath wrought,
  And grace shall wear the crown.

O may I practically shew
  My int'rest in that grace!
Be all I am, and have, and do,
  Devoted to thy praise!

A Select Collection of Hymns, ed. by the Countess of Huntingdon,
1780

John Berridge. 1716–1793

"I will clothe thee with change of raiment,"

Zach. iii. 4

Dress uniform the soldiers wear,
  When duty calls abroad,
Not purchas'd at their cost or care,
  But by the prince bestow'd.

Christ's soldiers too, if Christ-like bred,
  Have regimental dress,
'Tis linen white and fac'd with red,
  'Tis Christ's own righteousness.

A rich and sightly robe it is,
  And to the soldiers dear;
No rose can learn to blush like this,
  Nor lily look so fair.

No wit of man could weave this robe,
    'Tis of such texture fine;
Nor could the wealth of all the globe
    By purchase make it mine.

The robe was wrought by Jesu's hand,
    And dy'd in his own blood;
And all the cherubs gazing stand
    To view this robe of God.

Tho' worn, it never waxeth old,
    No spots upon it fall,
It makes a soldier brisk and bold,
    And dutiful withal.

Array me in this robe complete,
    For this will hide my shame,
And make me sing, and make me fight,
    And bless my captain's name.

Sion's Songs, or Hymns, 1785

Anonymous

AN HYMN

Almighty Lord! dispose each mind
To seek the good of human kind:
Teach us with others' joys to glow;
Teach us to feel for others' woe.

Recitative

Ye, who by heaven's protecting care,
Have happ'ly 'scap'd temptation's snare:
'Tis your's to hide a daughter's shame;
'Tis your's to guard a sister's fame.

Solo

In that torn breast which heaves with sighs,
What fierce contending passions rise!
Timely suppress the fatal strife,
And save the harmless infant's life.

Duet

Behold in misery's dreary shade,
The widow, with her children, laid:
Hear them with piteous moan, deplore
Husband and father now no more.

Solo

The helpless babe, by hunger prest,
Clings to the famish'd mother's breast:
In vain it ev'ry effort tries;
Life's fountains yield it no supplies.

Chorus

Thanks be to GOD, who heard our cry,
When not one earthly friend was nigh!
To Him our voices let us raise,
In songs of gratitude and praise.

Hallelujah! Amen.

The Foundling Hospital Collection, 1798

Rowland Hill. 1744–1833

AGAINST PRIDE IN DRESS
Be ye clothed with humility. 2 Pet. v. 5

Angels are happy, cloath'd with wings,
But our new clothes are dang'rous things;
The child well dress'd, had need beware,
Lest his fine raiment prove a snare.

Adam in innocence attir'd,
Was lovely; yet not self-admired:
But we from garments, made to hide
Mis'ry and shame, can gather pride.

A tatter'd coat were better far,
Than all the ornaments that are;
If sinners cannot e'en be neat,
But they must swell with self-conceit.

And what are children at the best,
But beggars charitably dress'd?
Poor little beggars, who receive
Nothing but what their parents give.

But happy children, they whose dress
Is the Redeemer's righteousness;
E'er long in glory they shall shine,
Rob'd in that raiment all divine.

*Divine Hymns attempted in easy language for the use of children
Designed as an appendix to Dr. Watts Divine Songs, 1790.*

ADMIRATION OF THE LOVE OF CHRIST

The fairest of ten thousand fairs,
Bends down his chariot from the skies;
Infinite grace his way prepares,
Infinite love adorns his eyes.

O! 'tis a thought would melt a rock,
And make a heart of iron move,
That those sweet lips, that heavenly look,
Could seek and wish a mortal love!

When, as a traitor doom'd to fire,
I stood condemn'd to endless pains;
He flew on wings of strong desire,
Assum'd my guilt, and took my chains.

Did pity ever stoop so low,
Dress'd in divinity and blood?
Was ever rebel courted so
In groans of an expiring God?

Now may my tongue in ceaseless praise
Make known the wonders he hath done;
May all my heart admire his grace,
And all my life be his alone.

LUKE XXIV. 31

No farther go tonight, but stay,
        Dear Saviour, 'till the break of day,
    Turn in, dear Lord, with me;
And in the morning, when I wake,
Me in thine arms, my Jesus, take,
        And I'll go on with thee.

A Collection of Psalms and Hymns, 1798

MINOR SECTS PART II
1757–1794

THE INGHAMITES

Anonymous

While my Jesus I'm possessing,
    Great's the happiness I know:
While his corpse I am caressing,
    Sweetest odours round me flow:
Happy I'm in his embraces,
    Proving all his kisses sweet;
Singing never-ceasing praises,
    Mary-like before his feet.

Oh! how happy are the moments,
    Which I here in transport spend;
Life deriving from his torments,
    Who remains the sinner's Friend:
Here I'll sit for ever viewing
    How the blood flows from each vein;
Ev'ry stream, my soul bedewing,
    Mortifies the carnal flame.

Really blessed is the portion
    Destin'd me by sov'reign grace;
Still to view divine compassion
    In the Saviour's bruised face:
'Tis my fixed resolution
    Jesus Christ my Lord to love;
At his feet to fix my station,
    Nor from thence a hair's breadth move.

Here it is I find my heaven,
    While upon my lamb I gaze;
Love I much, I've more forgiven;
    I'm a miracle of grace:
Fill'd with sinner-like contrition,
    With my tears his feet I'll bathe;
Happy in the sweet fruition
    Of my Saviour's painful death.

From his pierc'd and wounded body
    Issu'd streams of sacred gore;
From his hands and feet so bloody
    Flow'd a medicine for each sore:
From his side, that fountain precious,
    Pardons with the blood did flow;
This to taste is most delicious,
    Causing all within to glow.

May I still enjoy this feeling,
    In all need to Jesu go;
Prove his wounds each day more healing,
    And from hence salvation draw:
May I have the spirit's unction
    Filling me with holy shame;
Still retain a close connection
    With the person of the Lamb.

A Collection of Hymns for the use of those that seek, and those that have Redemption in the Blood of Christ, 1757

THE MUGGLETONIANS

Boyer Glover. fl. 1770

SONG

Oh! what great and glorious treasure,
 Flow within my soul, I see;
Now I know by true repentance,
 What it was that died for me;
The Godhead spirit here did centre,
 In a human frame I see;
The whole Godhead here did enter
 Into silent death for me.
  The Godhead, &c.

Altho' I am a wicked sinner,
 And justly do deserve to die;
Within my soul mercy is crying,
 You're blest, you live eternally;
Like faithful Noah, I great favor
 In the sight of God have found;
His precious blood, that glorious Saviour,
 Has heal'd the serpent's deadly wound.
  Like faithful &c.

Oh! how my soul is freed from sorrow,
 Now I by faith my God can see;
While curs'd devils fill'd with horror,
 Dread the great eternity;
When my soul was almost dying,
 By reason's malice great to me;
In my soul a voice was crying,
 Oh! my God hath died for me.
  When my, &c.

What tho' I live with cursed devils,
  And amongst them here shall die;
I shall have a glorious supper,
  When my God comes from on high;
On the flesh of mighty captains,
  With my God, I then shall feed;
On mighty men of that great nation,
  Which caus'd our glorious God to bleed.
    On the, &c.

And on the flesh of smaller devils,
  I shall feed by faith, I see;
When my God comes in that morning,
  Of the great eternity,
Kings and priests will lose their power,
  None will bear supremacy;
All fill'd with horror in that hour,
  They'll be damn'd eternally.
    Kings and, &c.

When upon them we are feeding,
  With our glorious God divine,
And do know they are a bleeding,
  Oh! how glorious we shall shine;
Fill'd with love and grateful praises,
  With acclamations loud will cry,
When our God from death us raises,
  Into blest eternity.
    Fill'd with, &c.

Divine Songs of the Muggletonians, 1829

THE BEREANS

John Barclay. 1734–1798

The Sons of God! entrancing love!
    Lift up thine eyes, and see
Love show'ring down from all above,
    Love show'ring down on thee!
The heav'ns bow'd down to meet the earth,
    Jehovah bow'd them low;
He smote the sin, he smote the death,
    And dash'd them with his bow.

He quell'd the lion's keenest fire,
    The dragon's fiery glare;
The dragon flew before his ire,
    The lion crouch'd for fear:
He bound their paws in wreathed chains;
    In wreathed chains they roll;
The brimstone-billow o'er them reigns,
    In boiling lakes they growl.

These were the foes that pluck'd us down,
    That pluck'd us from the sky;
They rent our robes, they tore our crown;
    (Trampled in blood we lie).
Our blood they suck'd, they crush'd our bones,
    They crush'd us in the earth.
Destruction fierce, with havock reigns;
    Sin havocks us to death.

Jehovah view'd them, view'd his Son,
    And view'd the mangled prey—
The Son in lightning fires flew down,
    With bolts the fiends to fray—

They saw the tempest on its way,
    In winged whirlwinds rowl;
They shriek, they roar, they gnash, they bray,
    Bruis'd thro' their inmost soul.

But, lo, he breathed on our bones,
    His Spirit breathed love;
And now we bloom his living sons,
    Born of the Holy Dove.
The Holy Dove with heavn'ly loves,
    Soft hov'ring o'er our joys,
With kindly influences moves,
    And ev'ry grief destroys.

A CHILD'S DREAM*

Know ye who I saw last night,
    Sleeping on my bed, mamma?
A shining creature all in light;
    She seem'd a heav'nly maid, mamma.
I met her tripping o'er the dew,
    Fine as a queen of May, mamma;
She saw, she smil'd, she to me flew,
    And bade me come away, mamma.

I look'd, I lov'd, I blush'd a while;
    O how could I say No, mamma?
She spoke so sweet, so sweet did smile,
    I was oblig'd to go, mamma;
For love my tender heart beguil'd,
    I felt unusual flames, mamma;
My infant-fancy turn'd so wild,
    So strangly wild my dreams, mamma.

* If this song is supposed to need any apology, the publisher honestly acknowledges, that he has none other but this to offer, viz., that it is founded, as to the substance of it, upon fact.

I was, I was, I know not how,
 O had you been with me, mamma!
Such wonders open'd to our view,
 As none but angels see, mamma.
Methought we wander'd in a grove,
 A grove in pleasant fields, mamma;
In joyful measures on we move,
 As music rapture yields, mamma.

She took me in her snow-white hand,
 Then led me through the air, mamma,
Far higher above sea and land,
 Than ever eagles were, mamma!
The sea and land, with all their store
 Of rivers, woods, and hills, mamma,
Indeed they did appear no more
 Than five of doctor's pills, mamma.

I sought, and sought pappa's estate,
 But found it not at all, mamma;
The world, in whole, seem'd not so great
 As half a cannon ball, mamma.
We saw the sun but like a star,
 The moon a mustard-seed, mamma;
Like Elias in his fiery car,
 All-wing'd with lightning's speed, mamma.

Swift as our thoughts, O joyful day!
 We glanc'd thro' all the spheres, mamma;
Their music sounding by the way,
 Heav'n rush'd upon our ears, mamma;
Now spheres, and all we knew before,
 Are lost unto our view, mamma;
The former things are now no more;
 Behold, all things are new, mamma.

No death there is, nor sorrow there,
    To damnify our bliss, mamma;
For death, sin, hell, and sorrow, are
    Deep-buried in th' abyss, mamma.
With wintry storms the ground ne'er pines,
    Cloth'd in eternal bloom, mamma;
For there the Sun of glory shines;
    And all the just with him, mamma.

I saw my sister Anna shine,
    A virgin in her prime, mamma;
Not such as with you sometimes dine,
    But like the angels fine, mamma;
Her robe was all a flowing stream
    Of silver dipt in light, mamma:
But ah! it wak'd me from my dream,
    It shin'd so strong and bright, mamma!

A Select Collection of New Original Spiritual Songs, 1776

THE GLASSITES

William Leighton

SONG

With ravish'd eyes, Lord, we admire
    These radiant curtains of thy throne!
Wide heav'n, adorn'd with studs of fire,
    Proclaims Omnipotence alone:
These shining watchers, in their silent talk,
Proclaim thy glory, proclaim thy glory,
    In their evening walk.

182

The purple morn, with gilded ray,
    Renews the day with glad'ning light;
Th' o'erjoy'd creation welcomes day,
    With cheerful motion, till the night
To silent slumbers hush the lab'ring ball:
These preach thy glory, these preach thy glory,
        Thro' the spacious all.

Array'd with light, in silver streams,
    Thron'd in his fiery tend, the sun,
Diffusing all enliv'ning beams,
    Round heav'n's extremities doth run;
Swift as a racer, as a bridegroom gay,
In pride of glory, in pride of glory,
        Constituting day.

His genial warmth, the world immense
    Confesses, in each fruit and flow'r;
Thou mak'st his brooding influence
    Feast thy creation ev'ry hour:
Thou mad'st him this great world's both eye and soul,
Sole vital spirit, sole vital spirit,
        Known from pole to pole.

Art dimly paints that brilliant ball;
    That's but an emblem faint, to shew
The sun of righteousness, where all
    The beams of God shine forth most true.
With rays diffus'd, in healing words he glows,
And circling warms, and circling warms
        The nations as he goes.

Tho' blinded reas'ners mark thee not,
    In nature's wide amazing scene,
Where all thy labours point thee out,
    And all thy footsteps shew so plain

Thy pow'r, and godhead, to earth's utmost line,
Where brighter rays, where brighter rays
  Of God ne'er deign'd to shine;

Yet ravish'd, with sublime delight,
  Believers view in ev'ry line
Of thy pure oracles, the light
  Of truth, and mercy all divine:
Thy law, and law fulfill'd, these testify,
Convert the soul, convert the soul,
  And bow the heart to thee.

Christian Songs, 1794.

THE NINETEENTH CENTURY
1820–1908

Thomas Moore. 1779–1852

THE TURF SHALL BE MY FRAGRANT SHRINE

The turf shall be my fragrant shrine;
My temple, Lord! that Arch of thine;
My censer's breath the mountain airs,
And silent thoughts my only prayers.

My choir shall be the moonlight waves,
When murm'ring homeward to their caves,
Or when the stillness of the sea,
E'en more than music, breathes of Thee!

I'll seek, by day, some glade unknown,
All light and silence, like thy Throne!
And the pale stars shall be, at night,
The only eyes that watch my rite.

Thy Heaven, on which 'tis bliss to look,
Shall be my pure and shining Book,
Where I shall read, in words of flame,
The glories of thy wondrous Name.

I'll read thy Anger in the rack
That clouds awhile the day-beam's track;
Thy mercy in the azure hue
Of sunny brightness, breaking through!

There's nothing bright, above, below,
From flowers that bloom to stars that glow,
But in its light my soul can see
Some feature of thy Deity!

There's nothing dark, below, above,
But in its gloom I trace thy Love,
And meekly wait that moment, when
Thy touch shall turn all bright again!

AS DOWN IN THE SUNLESS RETREATS

As down in the sunless retreats of the Ocean,
   Sweet flowers are springing no mortal can see,
So, deep in my soul the still prayer of devotion,
   Unheard by the world, rises silent to Thee;
      My God! silent, to Thee;
      Pure, warm, silent, to Thee.—
So, deep in my soul the still prayer of devotion,
   Unheard by the world, rises silent to Thee.

As still, to the star of its worship, tho' clouded,
   The needle points faithfully o'er the dim sea,
So, dark as I roam, in this wintry world shrouded,
   The hope of my spirit turns trembling to Thee;
      My God! trembling, to Thee;
      True, fond, trembling, to Thee;—
So, dark as I roam, in this wintry world shrouded,
   The hope of my spirit turns trembling to Thee.

Sacred Songs, 1820

John Keble. 1792–1866

MORNING

His compassions fail not; they are new every morning
Lament. iii. 22, 23

Hues of the rich unfolding morn,
That, ere the glorious sun be born,
By some soft touch invisible
Around his path are taught to dwell;—

Thou rustling breeze so fresh and gay,
That dancest forth at opening day,
And brushing by with joyous wing,
Wakenest each little leaf to sing;—

Ye fragrant clouds of dewy steam,
By which deep grove and tangled stream
Pay, for soft rains in season given,
Their tribute to the genial heaven;—

Why waste your treasures of delight
Upon our thankless, joyous sight;
Who day by day to sin awake,
Seldom of heaven and you partake?

Oh! timely happy, timely wise,
Hearts that with rising morn arise!
Eyes that the beam celestial view,
Which evermore makes all things new!*

New every morning is the love
Our wakening and uprising prove;
Through sleep and darkness safely brought,
Restored to life, and power, and thought.

New mercies, each returning day,
Hover around us while we pray;
New perils past, new sins forgiven,
New thoughts of God, new hopes of heaven.

If on our daily course our mind
Be set to hallow all we find,
New treasures still, of countless price,
God will provide for sacrifice.

* Revelations xxi. 5.

Old friends, old scenes, will lovelier be,
As more of heaven in each we see:
Some softening gleam of love and prayer
Shall dawn on every cross and care.

As for some dear familiar strain
Untir'd we ask, and ask again,
Ever, in its melodious store,
Finding a spell unheard before;

Such is the bliss of souls serene,
When they have sworn, and stedfast mean,
Counting the cost, in all to' espy
Their God, in all themselves deny.

O could we learn that sacrifice,
What lights would all around us rise!
How would our hearts with wisdom talk
Along Life's dullest dreariest walk!

We need not bid, for cloister'd cell,
Our neighbour and our work farewell,
Nor strive to wind ourselves too high
For sinful man beneath the sky:

The trivial round, the common task,
Would furnish all we ought to ask;
Room to deny ourselves; a road
To bring us, daily, nearer God.

Seek we no more; content with these,
Let present Rapture, Comfort, Ease,
As Heaven shall bid them, come and go:—
The secret this of Rest below.

Only, O Lord, in thy dear love
Fit us for perfect Rest above;
And help us, this and every day,
To live more nearly as we pray.

EVENING

Abide with us, for it is towards evening, and the day is far spent.
St. Luke xxiv. 29.

'Tis gone, that bright and orbed blaze,
Fast fading from our wistful gaze;
Yon mantling cloud has hid from sight
The last faint pulse of quivering light.

In darkness and in weariness
The traveller on his way must press,
No gleam to watch on tree or tower,
Whiling away the lonesome hour.

Sun of my soul! Thou Saviour dear,
It is not night if Thou be near:
Oh may no earth-bound cloud arise
To hide Thee from thy servant's eyes.

When round thy wondrous works below
My searching rapturous glance I throw,
Tracing out Wisdom, Power, and Love,
In earth or sky, in stream or grove;—

Or by the light thy words disclose
Watch Time's full river as it flows,
Scanning thy gracious Providence,
Where not too deep for mortal sense:—

When with dear friends sweet talk I hold,
And all the flowers of life unfold;—
Let not my heart within me burn,
Except in all I Thee discern.

When the soft dews of kindly sleep
My wearied eyelids gently steep,
Be my last thought, how sweet to rest
For ever on my Saviour's breast.

Abide with me from morn till eve,
For without Thee I cannot live:
Abide with me when night is nigh,
For without Thee I dare not die.

Thou Framer of the light and dark,
Steer through the tempest thine own ark:
Amid the howling wintry sea
We are in port if we have Thee.*

The Rulers of this Christian land,
'Twixt Thee and us ordained to stand,—
Guide Thou their course, O Lord, aright,
Let all do all as in thy sight.

Oh by thine own sad burthen, borne
So meekly up the hill of scorn,
Teach Thou thy Priests their daily cross
To bear as thine, nor count it loss!

If some poor wandering soul of thine
Have spurn'd, to-day, the voice divine,
Now, Lord, the gracious work begin;
Let her no more lie down in sin.

Watch by the sick: enrich the poor
With blessings from thy boundless store:
Be every mourner's sleep to-night
Like infant's slumbers, pure and light.

Come near and bless us when we wake,
Ere through the world our way we take:
Till in the ocean of thy love
We lose ourselves in heaven above.

* Then they willingly received Him into the ship: and immediately
the ship was at the land whither they went. *St. John.* vi. 21

The Christian Year, 1827

Reginald Heber. 1783–1826

The Lord will come! the earth shall quake,
The hills their fixed seat forsake;
And, withering, from the vault of night
The stars withdraw their feeble light.

The Lord will come! but not the same
As once in lowly form he came,
A silent lamb to slaughter led,
The bruis'd, the suffering, and the dead.

The Lord will come! a dreadful form,
With wreath of flame, and robe of storm,
On cherub wings, and wings of wind,
Anointed Judge of human-kind!

Can this be He who wont to stray
A pilgrim on the world's highway;
By Power oppress'd, and mock'd by Pride?
Oh God! is this the crucified?

Go, tyrants! to the rocks complain!
Go, seek the mountain's cleft in vain!
But Faith, victorious o'er the tomb,
Shall sing for joy—the Lord is come!

EPIPHANY.—NO. 2

Brightest and best of the sons of the morning!
Dawn on our darkness and lend us thine aid!
Star of the East, the horizon adorning,
Guide where our infant Redeemer is laid!

Cold on his cradle the dew-drops are shining,
    Low lies his head with the beasts of the stall,
Angels adore him in slumber reclining,
    Maker and Monarch and Saviour of all!

Say, shall we yield him, in costly devotion,
    Odours of Edom and offerings divine?
Gems of the mountain and pearls of the ocean,
    Myrrh from the forest or gold from the mine?

Vainly we offer each ample oblation;
    Vainly with gifts would his favour secure:
Richer by far is the heart's adoration;
    Dearer to God are the prayers of the poor.

Brightest and best of the sons of the morning!
    Dawn on our darkness and lend us thine aid!
Star of the East, the horizon adorning,
    Guide where our infant Redeemer is laid.

FIRST SUNDAY AFTER EPIPHANY.—NO. 2

By cool Siloam's shady rill
    How sweet the lily grows!
How sweet the breath beneath the hill
    Of Sharon's dewy rose!

Lo such the child whose early feet
    The paths of peace have trod;
Whose secret heart, with influence sweet,
    Is upward drawn to God!

By cool Siloam's shady rill
    The lily must decay;
The rose that blooms beneath the hill
    Must shortly fade away.

And soon, too soon, the wintry hour
    Of man's maturer age
Will shake the soul with sorrow's power,
    And stormy passion's rage!

O Thou, whose infant feet were found
    Within thy Father's shrine!
Whose years with changeless virtue crown'd,
    Were all alike Divine.

Dependant on thy bounteous breath,
    We seek thy grace alone,
In childhood, manhood, age, and death,
    To keep us still thine own!

FOURTH SUNDAY AFTER EPIPHANY.—NO. 4

When through the torn sail the wild tempest is streaming,
When o'er the dark wave the red lightning is gleaming,
Nor hope lends a ray the poor seaman to cherish,
We fly to our Maker—"Help, Lord! or we perish!"

O Jesus! once toss'd on the breast of the billow,
Aroused by the shriek of despair from thy pillow,
Now, seated in glory, the mariner cherish,
Who cries in his danger—"Help, Lord! or we perish!"

And oh, when the whirlwind of passion is raging,
When hell in our heart his wild warfare is waging,
Arise in thy strength thy redeemed to cherish,
Rebuke the destroyer—"Help, Lord! or we perish!"

FOURTH SUNDAY IN LENT

Oh King of earth and air and sea!
The hungry ravens cry to Thee:
To Thee the scaly tribes that sweep
The bosom of the boundless deep;

To Thee the lions roaring call,
The common Father, kind to all!
Then grant Thy servants, Lord! we pray,
Our daily bread from day to day!

The fishes may for food complain;
The ravens spread their wings in vain;
The roaring lions lack and pine;
But, God! Thou carest still for thine!

Thy bounteous hand with food can bless
The bleak and lonely wilderness;
And Thou hast taught us, Lord! to pray
For daily bread from day to day!

And oh, when through the wilds we roam
That part us from from our heavenly home:
When, lost in danger, want, and woe,
Our faithless tears begin to flow;

Do Thou Thy gracious comfort give,
By which alone the soul may live;
And grant Thy servants, Lord! we pray,
The bread of life from day to day!

TRINITY SUNDAY

Holy, holy, holy, Lord God Almighty!
  Early in the morning our song shall rise to Thee;
Holy, holy, holy! merciful and mighty!
  God in three persons, blessed Trinity!

Holy, holy, holy! all the saints adore Thee,
  Casting down their golden crowns around the glassy sea;
Cherubim and seraphim falling down before Thee,
  Which wert and art and evermore shalt be!

194

Holy, holy, holy! Though the darkness hide Thee,
  Though the eye of sinful man Thy glory may not see,
Only Thou art holy, there is none beside Thee,
  Perfect in power, in love, and purity!

Holy, holy, holy, Lord God Almighty!
  All Thy works shall praise Thy name, in earth and sky
        and sea;
Holy, holy, holy! merciful and mighty!
  God in three persons, blessed Trinity!

FIRST SUNDAY AFTER TRINITY.—NO. I

Room for the Proud! Ye sons of clay
From far his sweeping pomp survey,
Nor, rashly curious, clog the way
      His chariot wheels before!

Lo! with what scorn his lofty eye
Glances o'er Age and Poverty,
And bids intruding Conscience fly
      Far from his palace door!

Room for the Proud! but slow the feet
That bear his coffin down the street:
And dismal seems his winding-sheet
      Who purple lately wore!

Ah! where must now his spirit fly
In naked, trembling agony?
Or how shall he for mercy cry,
      Who shew'd it not before!

Room for the Proud! in ghastly state
The lords of Hell his coming wait,
And flinging wide the dreadful gate,
      That shuts to ope no more.

"Lo here with us the seat," they cry,
"For him who mock'd at poverty,
And bade intruding Conscience fly
Far from his palace door!"

BEFORE A COLLECTION MADE FOR THE SOCIETY FOR THE PROPAGATION OF THE GOSPEL

From Greenland's icy mountains,
From India's coral strand,
Where Afric's sunny fountains
Roll down their golden sand;
From many an ancient river,
From many a palmy plain,
They call us to deliver
Their land from error's chain!

What though the spicy breezes
Blow soft o'er Java's isle,
Though every prospect pleases,
And only man is vile:
In vain with lavish kindness
The gifts of God are strewn,
The Heathen, in his blindness,
Bows down to wood and stone!

Can we, whose souls are lighted
With Wisdom from on high,
Can we to men benighted
The lamp of life deny?
Salvation! oh, Salvation!
The joyful sound proclaim,
Till each remotest nation
Has learn'd Messiah's name!

Waft waft ye winds his story,
 And you ye waters roll,
Till like a sea of glory,
 It spreads from pole to pole;
Till o'er our ransom'd Nature,
 The Lamb for sinners slain,
Redeemer, King, Creator,
 In bliss returns to reign.

Heber's Hymns, 1827

Henry Hart Milman. 1791–1868

SECOND SUNDAY IN ADVENT.—NO. 2

The chariot! the chariot! its wheels on fire
As the Lord cometh down in the pomp of his ire:
Self-moving it drives on its pathway of cloud,
And the Heavens with the burthen of Godhead are bow'd.

The glory! the glory! by myriads are pour'd
The hosts of the Angels to wait on their Lord,
And the glorified saints and the martyrs are there,
And all who the palm-wreath of victory wear!

The trumpet! the trumpet! the dead have all heard:
Lo the depths of the stone-cover'd charnel are stirr'd:
From the sea, from the land, from the south and the north,
The vast generations of man are come forth.

The judgement! the judgement! the thrones are all set,
Where the Lamb and the white vested Elders are met!
All flesh is at once in the sight of the Lord,
And the doom of eternity hangs on his word!

Oh mercy! oh mercy! look down from above,
Creator! on us thy sad children, with love!
When beneath to their darkness the wicked are driven,
May our sanctified souls find a mansion in heaven!

SIXTH SUNDAY IN LENT.—NO. I

Ride on! ride on in majesty!
Hark! all the tribes Hosanna cry!
Thine humble beast pursues his road,
With palms and scatter'd garments strew'd!

Ride on! ride on in majesty!
In lowly pomp ride on to die!
Oh Christ! Thy triumphs now begin
O'er captive Death and conquer'd Sin!

Ride on! ride on in majesty!
The winged squadrons of the sky
Look down with sad and wondering eyes,
To see the approaching sacrifice!

Ride on! ride on in majesty!
Thy last and fiercest strife is nigh;
The Father on his sapphire throne
Expects His own anointed Son!

Ride on! ride on in majesty!
In lowly pomp ride on to die!
Bow Thy meek head to mortal pain!
Then take, oh God! Thy power, and reign!

H. H. MILMAN   *Heber's Hymns, 1827*

John Henry Newman. 1801–1890

THE PILLAR OF THE CLOUD

Lead, Kindly Light, amid the encircling gloom,
　Lead Thou me on!
The night is dark, and I am far from home—
　Lead Thou me on!
Keep Thou my feet; I do not ask to see
The distant scene,—one step enough for me.

I was not ever thus, nor pray'd that Thou
    Shouldst lead me on.
I loved to choose and see my path; but now
    Lead Thou me on!
I loved the garish day, and, spite of fears,
Pride ruled my will: remember not past years.

So long Thy power hath blest me, sure it still
    Will lead me on,
O'er moor and fen, o'er crag and torrent, till
    The night is gone;
And with the morn those angel faces smile
Which I have loved long since, and lost awhile.

          At sea. June 16th, 1833
          Verses on various occasions, 1868

Henry Francis Lyte. 1793–1847

AUTUMNAL HYMN

The leaves around me falling
    Are preaching of decay;
The hollow winds are calling,
    "Come, pilgrim, come away!"
The day, in night declining,
    Says, I must too decline:
The year its life resigning—
    Its lot foreshadows mine.

The light my path surrounding,
    The loves to which I cling,
The hopes within me bounding,
    The joys that round me wing—
All, all, like stars at even,
    Just gleam, and shoot away;
Pass on before to heaven,
    And chide at my delay.

The friends gone there before me
    Are calling me from high,
And joyous angels o'er me
    Tempt sweetly to the sky.
"Why wait," they say, "and wither
    "'Mid scenes of death and sin?
"O rise to glory hither,
    "And find true life begin!"

I hear the invitation,
    And fain would rise and come—
A sinner, to salvation;
    An exile, to his home:
But while I here must linger,
    Thus, thus, let all I see
Point on, with faithful finger,
    To heaven, O Lord, and Thee.

THE PILGRIM'S SONG

There remaineth a rest for the people of God. Heb. iv

My rest is in heaven; my rest is not here;
Then why should I murmur when trials are near?
Be hushed, my dark spirit! the worst that can come
But shortens thy journey, and hastens thee home.

It is not for me to be seeking my bliss
And building my hopes in a region like this:
I look for a city which hands have not piled;
I pant for a country by sin undefiled.

The thorn and the thistle around me may grow;
I would not lie down upon roses below:
I ask not my portion, I seek not a rest,
Till I find them for ever in Jesus's breast.

Afflictions may damp me, they cannot destroy;
One glimpse of His love turns them all into joy:
And the bitterest tears, if He smile but on them,
Like dew in the sunshine, grow diamond and gem.

Let doubt then and danger, my progress oppose;
They only make heaven more sweet at the close.
Come joy, or come sorrow, whate'er may befal,
An hour with my God will make up for it all.

A scrip on my back, and a staff in my hand,
I march on in haste through an enemy's land:
The road may be rough, but it cannot be long;
And I'll smooth it with hope, and cheer it with song.

Poems, Chiefly Religious, 1833

ABIDE WITH ME

Abide with us: for it is toward evening, and the day is far spent.
Luke xxiv. 29

Abide with me! Fast falls the Eventide;
The darkness deepens: Lord, with me abide!
When other helpers fail, and comforts flee,
Help of the helpless, O abide with me!

Swift to its close ebbs out life's little day;
Earth's joys grow dim; its glories pass away:
Change and decay in all around I see;
O Thou, who changest not, abide with me!

Not a brief glance I beg, a passing word,
But as Thou dwell'st with Thy disciples, Lord,
Familiar, condescending, patient, free,
Come, not to sojourn, but abide, with me!

Come not in terrors, as the King of Kings;
But kind and good, with healing in Thy wings:
Tears for all woes, a heart for every plea.
Come, Friend of Sinners, and thus bide with me!

Thou on my head in early youth didst smile,
And, though rebellious and perverse meanwhile,
Thou hast not left me, oft as I left Thee.
On to the close, O Lord, abide with me!

I need thy presence every passing hour.
What but thy grace can foil the Tempter's power?
Who like Thyself my guide and stay can be?
Through cloud and sunshine, O abide with me!

I fear no foe with Thee at hand to bless:
Ills have no weight, and tears no bitterness.
Where is death's sting? where, grave, thy victory?
I triumph still, if Thou abide with me.

Hold then Thy cross before my closing eyes;
Shine through the gloom, and point me to the skies:
Heaven's morning breaks, and earth's vain shadows flee.
In life in death, O Lord, abide with me!

Remains, 1850

Sir Robert Grant. 1779–1838

GLORY AND GOODNESS OF GOD

O Worship the King all glorious above!
O gratefully sing his power and his love!
Our Shield and Defender—the Ancient of days,
Pavilion'd in splendor, and girded with praise.
O tell of his might, O sing of his grace!
Whose robe is the light—whose canopy space,
His chariots of wrath the deep thunder-clouds form,
And dark is his path on the wings of the storm.

The earth with its store of wonders untold,
Almighty! thy power hath founded of old;
Hath stablish'd it fast by a changeless decree,
And round it hath cast like a mantle the sea.
Thy bountiful care what tongue can recite?
It breathes in the air—it shines in the light;
In streams from the hills it descends to the plain;
And sweetly distils in the dew and the rain.

Frail children of dust, and feeble as frail,
In thee do we trust, nor find thee to fail;
Thy mercies how tender, how firm to the end,
Our Maker, Defender, Redeemer, and Friend!
O measureless Might—ineffable Love!
While angels delight to hymn thee above,
They humbler creation, though feeble their lays,
With true adoration shall lisp to thy praise.

H. V. Elliot's Psalms and Hymns, 1835

James Montgomery. 1771–1854

AT HOME IN HEAVEN
1 Thess. iv. 17

Part I

"For ever with the Lord!"
    —Amen; so let it be;
Life from the dead is in that word,
    'Tis immortality.

Here in the body pent,
    Absent from Him I roam;
Yet nightly pitch my moving tent
    A day's march nearer home.

My Father's house on high,
        Home of my soul, how near,
At times, to faith's foreseeing eye,
        Thy golden gates appear!

Ah! then my spirit faints
        To reach the land I love,
The bright inheritance of saints,
        Jerusalem above.

Yet clouds will intervene,
        And all my prospect flies,
Like Noah's dove, I flit between
        Rough seas and stormy skies.

Anon the clouds dispart,
        The winds and waters cease,
While sweetly o'er my gladden'd heart
        Expands the bow of peace.

Beneath its glowing arch,
        Along the hallow'd ground,
I see cherubic armies march,
        A camp of fire around.

I hear at morn and even,
        At noon and midnight hour,
The choral harmonies of heaven
        Earth's Babel-tongues o'erpower.

Then, then I feel that He,
        (Remember'd or forgot,)
The Lord is never far from me,
        Though I perceive Him not.

Part II

In darkness as in light,
    Hidden alike from view,
I sleep, I wake within *his* sight,
    Who looks existence through.

From the dim hour of birth,
    Through every changing state
Of mortal pilgrimage on earth,
    Till its appointed date;

All that I am, have been,
    All that I yet may be,
He sees at once, as He hath seen,
    And shall for ever see.

How can I meet His eyes?
    Mine on the cross I cast,
And own my life a Saviour's prize,
    Mercy from first to last.

"For ever with the Lord!"
    —Father, if 'tis thy will,
The promise of that faithful word,
    Even here to me fulfil.

Be thou at my right hand,
    Then can I never fail;
Uphold Thou me, and I shall stand,
    Fight, and I must prevail.

So when my latest breath
    Shall rend the veil in twain,
By death I shall escape from death,
    And life eternal gain.

Knowing as I am known,
    How shall I love that word,
And oft repeat before the throne,
    "For ever with the Lord!"

Then though the soul enjoy
    Communion high and sweet,
While worms this body must destroy,
    Both shall in glory meet.

The trump of final doom
    Will speak the self-same word,
And heaven's voice thunder through the tomb,
    "For ever with the Lord!"

The tomb shall echo deep
    That death-awakening sound;
The saints shall hear it in their sleep,
    And answer from the ground.

Then upward as they fly,
    That resurrection-word
Shall be their shout of victory,
    "For ever with the Lord!"

That resurrection-word,
    That shout of victory,
Once more,—"For ever with the Lord!"
    Amen; so let it be.

A Poet's Portfolio; or Minor Poems: In Three Books, 1835

THE VALLEY OF THE SHADOW OF DEATH
Psalm xxiii. 4

Though I walk the downward shade,
    Deepening through the vale of death,
Yet I will not be afraid,
    But, with my departing breath,
I will glory in my GOD,
    In my Saviour I will trust,
Strengthen'd by His staff and rod,
    While this body fall to dust.

Soon on wings, on wings of love,
    My transported soul shall rise,
Like the home returning dove,
    Vanishing through boundless skies;
Then, where death shall be no more,
    Sin nor suffering e'er molest,
All my days of mourning o'er,
    In his presence I shall rest.

Original Hymns, 1853

Jane E. Leeson. 1807–1882

PRAYER TO THE GOOD SHEPHERD

Loving Shepherd of Thy sheep,
Keep Thy lamb, in safety keep;
Nothing can Thy power withstand;
None can pluck me from Thy hand.
Bought with blood, and bought for Thee,
Thine, and only thine, I'd be,
Holy, harmless, humble, mild,
Jesus Christ's obedient child.

Loving Saviour, Thou didst give
Thine own life that we might live;
And the hands outstretch'd to bless,
Bear the cruel nails' impress.
I would bless thee every day,
Gladly all Thy will obey,
Like Thy blessed ones above,
Happy in thy precious love.

Loving Shepherd, ever near,
Teach Thy lamb Thy voice to hear;
Suffer not my steps to stray
From the straight and narrow way.
Where Thou leadest I would go,
Walking in Thy steps below,
Till before my Father's throne,
I shall know as I am known.

CHILD'S THOUGHTS IN A CHURCHYARD

The stones of it are the place of sapphires, and it hath dust of gold.

Oh, gently, gently will I speak,
        And softly, softly tread,
Where in the church's peaceful shade,
With solemn words the dead are laid
        In their last, lowly bed.

It is not right, it is not kind,
        To pass regardless by,
Where, 'neath each daisy-blossom'd mound,
Brethren and sisters all around,
        In dreamless slumbers lie.

The dead we call them, yet they live,
    With us they hope and pray;
Oh, many a martyr asks, "How long?
Holy and true, O Lord, how long
    Or ere thy judgement day?"

That day when ev'ry secret thing
    Shall be brought forth to light,
When many a gem of purest ray,
That hidden in earth's bosom lay,
    Shall sparkle into sight.

Yes, earth has precious fruit in store,
    Immortal and divine,
For she hath dust of purest gold,
And sapphire stones of price untold,
    One day in heaven to shine.

The place where many a saint is laid,
    Is sure a hallow'd spot,
Not to be pass'd without a prayer,
For those whose bodies slumber there,
    Whom God forgetteth not.

So I will pray, "Lord Jesus, come,
    Come soon and with Thee bring
Thy sleeping saints, earth's precious trust;
Oh, bid the dwellers in the dust
    At length awake, and sing:

And, Saviour, when Thou makest up
    Thy jewels in that day,
In mercy own me too for Thine,
For ever in Thy crown to shine,
    With spotless heav'n-lit ray."

Hymns and Scenes of Childhood, 1842; from second edition, 1848

John Chandler. 1806–1876

DIVINE CRESCEBAS PUER

In stature grows the heavenly Child
    With death before his eyes;
A Lamb unblemished, meek and mild,
    Prepared for sacrifice.

The Son of God his glory hides
    With parents mean and poor:
And He who made the heaven abides
    In dwelling-place obscure.

Those mighty hands that stay the sky
    No earthly toil refuse,
And He who set the stars on high,
    An humble trade pursues.

He before whom the angels stand,
    At whose behest they fly,
Now yields himself to man's command,
    And lays his glory by.

The Father's name we loudly raise,
    The Son we all adore,
The Holy Ghost, one God, we praise
    Both now and evermore.

Translated from the original of J.-B. de Santeuil, 1630–97
Hymns of the Primitive Church, 1837

Isaac Williams. 1802–1865

COMMEMORATION OF APOSTLES AT MIDNIGHT

Who maketh the clouds His chariot: and walketh upon the wings of the wind: He maketh His angels spirits; and His ministers a flaming fire. Psalm civ.

"Supreme, quales, Arbiter."

Disposer Supreme,
    And Judge of the earth,
Who choosest for Thine
    The weak and the poor;
To frail earthen vessels,
    And things of no worth,
Entrusting Thy riches
    Which aye shall endure.

Those vessels soon fail,
    Though full of Thy light;
They at Thy decree
    Are broken and gone;
Then brightly appeareth
    The arm of Thy might,
As through the clouds breaking
    The lightnings have shone.

Like clouds are they borne
    To do Thy great will,
And swift as the winds
    About the world go:
All full of Thy Godhead,
    While earth lieth still,
They thunder, they lighten,
    The waters o'erflow.

They thunder—their sound
　　It is Christ the Lord!
Then Satan doth fear,
　　His citadels fall,
As when the dread trumpets
　　Went forth at Thy word,
And on the ground lieth
　　The Canaanites' wall.

O loud be Thy trump,
　　And stirring the sound,
To rouse us, O Lord,
　　From sin's deadly sleep;
May lights which Thou kindlest
　　In darkness around,
The dull soul awaken
　　Her vigils to keep!

All glory to Thee,
　　Who art hid from sight,
Yet fillest with love
　　The vast infinite;
And reveal'd to our aid
　　As One and yet Three,
Dost call us from afar
　　Thy glory to see.

ON THE BLESSED VIRGIN MARY

He that is mighty hath done to me great things, and holy is His name.
Luke i.
　　　"Ut sol decoro lumine."

As the sun
　　O'er misty shrouds,
When he walks
　　Upon the clouds:

Or as when
    The moon doth rise,
And refreshes
    All the skies;

Or as when
    The lily flower
Stands amid
    The vernal bower;

Or the water's
    Glassy face
Doth reflect
    The starry space;

Thus above
    All mothers shone
The mother of
    The Blessed One.

Hymns translated from the Parisian Breviary, 1839

John Mason Neale. 1818–1866

IN A SLEEPLESS NIGHT

O Thou, Who rising long before the day,
    Went'st forth to pray
On the cold mount, by weariness opprest,
    That we might rest
With Thee hereafter; though my lot denies
    Sleep to mine eyes,
Blessed REDEEMER, how can I repine,
    Remembering Thine?

O Thou, Who at the fourth watch of the night
    Did'st come in sight
Of Thine Apostles, toiling on the wave;
    And, swift to save
From peril and from fear, said'st, drawing nigh,
    "Peace! It is I!"
O still my thoughts, tempestuous as that sea,
    Speak peace to me!

O Thou, Who did'st not roughly chide Thy Saint
    With faith too faint
To walk the waters, but with outstretch'd Hand
    Did'st bid him stand;
My faith is weak: according to Thy Word,
    Help me, O LORD!
Afraid of every danger; not afraid
    To seek Thine aid!

Oh, give Thy servant patience, to be still,
    And bear Thy Will;
Courage, to venture wholly on the Arm
    That will not harm;
The wisdom, that will never let me stray
    Out of my way;
The Love that, now afflicting, knoweth best
    When I should rest!

Thy Time is not yet come. Enough for me!
    Thy Time will be
The safest and the best; and how can I
    Wish it more nigh?
If e'er Thou settest me among Thy Blest,
    Enough of rest!
Meanwhile, altho' Thou bidd'st my pains not cease,
    Grant me Thy Peace!

Hymns for the Sick, 1843

MICHAELMAS DAY

Around the throne of GOD, a band
Of Bright and Glorious Angels stand;
Sweet harps within their hands they hold,
And on their heads are crowns of gold.

Some wait around HIM, ready still
To sing HIS praise and do HIS will;
And some, when HE commands them, go
To guard HIS servants here below.

When GOD rain'd fire and brim-stone down
On Sodom, that ungodly town,
HIS servant then was not forgot,
For Angels came to bring out Lot.

When in the grave the SAVIOUR lay,
Two Angels roll'd the stone away:
Their garments were exceeding white,
Their faces shining as the light.

Thither the women came with fear;
'The LORD is risen,—HE is not here:
'Why seek ye then,' they gently said,
'The Living thus among the dead?'

Herod the King had fix'd a day
To take Saint Peter's life away;
The very night before, he slept
Bound with two chains, and safely kept:

Then came an Angel down by night,
And all at once the prison was bright:
He burst the gates, he broke the chain,
And wicked Herod's care was vain.

LORD, give THY angels every day
Command to guide us on our way;
And bid them every evening keep
Their watch around us while we sleep;

So shall no wicked thing draw near
To do us harm, or cause us fear;
And we shall dwell, when life is past,
With Angels round THY throne at last.

Hymns for Children, 1843

LAYING THE FIRST STONE OF A CHURCH

O LORD of Hosts, Whose glory fills
The bounds of the eternal hills,
And yet vouchsafes, in Christian lands,
To dwell in temples made with hands:

Grant that all we, who here today,
Rejoicing, this foundation lay,
May be in very deed Thine Own,
Built on the precious Corner-stone.

Endue the creatures with Thy grace
That shall adorn Thy dwelling-place;
The beauty of the oak and pine,
The gold and silver, make them Thine.

To Thee they all pertain; to Thee
The treasures of the earth and sea;
And when we bring them to Thy Throne,
We but present Thee with Thine own.

Endue the hearts that guide with skill;
Preserve the hands that work from ill;
That we, who these foundations lay,
May raise the topstone in its day.

Both now and ever, LORD, protect
The temple of Thine own elect;
Be Thou in them, and they in Thee,
O Ever-blessed TRINITY!

Hymns for the Young, 1845

HIC BREVE VIVITUR

For thee, O dear dear country!
    Mine eyes their vigils keep;
For very love, beholding
    Thy happy name, they weep.
The mention of thy glory
    Is unction to the breast,
And medicine in sickness,
    And love, and life and rest.
O one, O onely mansion!
    O Paradise of joy!
Where tears are ever banished,
    And smiles have no alloy;
Beside thy living waters,
    All plants are, great and small,
The cedar of the forest,
    The hyssop of the wall:
With jaspers glow thy bulwarks;
    Thy streets with emeralds blaze:
The sardius and the topaz
    Unite in thee their rays:
Thine ageless walls are bonded
    With amethyst unpriced:

Thy Saints build up its fabric,
    And the corner-stone is CHRIST.
The Cross is all thy splendour,
    The Crucified thy praise:
His laud and benediction
    Thy ransomed people raise:
JESUS, the Gem of Beauty,
    True GOD and Man, they sing:
The never-failing Garden,
    The ever-golden Ring:
The Door, the Pledge, the Husband,
    The Guardian of His Court:
The Day-star of Salvation,
    The Porter and the Port.
Thou hast no shore, fair ocean!
    Thou hast no time, bright day!
Dear fountain of refreshment
    To pilgrims far away!
Upon the Rock of Ages
    They raise the holy tower;
Thine is the victor's laurel,
    And Thine the golden dower.

From the Rhythm of Bernard of Morlaix, 1859

*   *   *

Christian! dost thou *see* them
    On the holy ground,
How the troops of Midian
    Prowl and prowl around?
Christian! up and smite them.
    Counting gain but loss:
Smite them by the merit
    Of the Holy Cross!

Christian! dost thou *feel* them,
    How they work within,
Striving, tempting, luring,
    Goading into sin?
Christian! never tremble!
    Never be down-cast!
Smite them by the virtue
    Of the Lenten fast!

Christian! dost thou *hear* them,
    How they speak thee fair?
Always fast and vigil?
    Always watch and prayer?
Christian! answer boldly:
    While I breathe I pray:
Peace shall follow battle,
    Night shall end in day.

"Well I know thy trouble,
    O My servant true;
Thou art very weary,—
    I was weary too;
But that toil shall make thee
    Some day, all Mine own,
But the end of sorrow
    Shall be near My Throne."

Translated from the Greek of St. Andrew of Crete. Hymns of the Eastern Church, 1862

Sarah Flower Adams. 1805–1848

Nearer, my God, to thee,
    Nearer to thee!
E'en though it be a cross
    That raiseth me:

Still all my song would be,
Nearer, my God, to thee—
        Nearer to thee!

Though like the wanderer,
        The sun gone down,
Darkness be over me,
        My rest a stone;
Yet in my dreams I'd be
Nearer, my God, to thee—
        Nearer to thee!

There let the way appear,
        Steps unto heaven;
All that thou send'st to me
        In mercy given;
Angels to beckon me
Nearer, my God, to thee—
        Nearer to thee!

Then with my waking thoughts
        Bright with thy praise,
Out of my stony griefs
        Bethel I'll raise:
So by my woes to be
Nearer, my God, to thee—
        Nearer to thee!

Or if on joyful wing
        Cleaving the sky,
Sun, moon, and stars forgot,
        Upwards I fly:
Still all my song shall be,
Nearer, my God, to thee—
        Nearer to thee!

Hymns and Anthems, ed. W. J. Fox, 1845

Thomas Kelly. 1769–1854

For I am a stranger with thee. Ps. xxxix.

I'm going home, detain me not;
　　I must not loiter by the way,
Lest night come on; for who knows what
　　Might happen then—I must not stay.

'Twould ill become the man who says,
　　He's passing thro', to be like those
Whose home is here. His words and ways,
　　Should with his pilgrim state agree.

I must not love the things that are;
　　They only lead the pilgrim wrong;
They draw him from his purpose far;
　　They take away his joy and song.

I must not stop, no matter what
　　May notice claim—I'm going home.
Be mine the weary pilgrim's lot.
　　'Tis labour now, but rest will come.

And rest to those that weary are,
　　Is sweet, but sweet to such alone;
The hope of rest is better far
　　Than if the world were all our own.

The pilgrims soon will gather'd be,
　　Within their father's house above:
A holy, happy family,
　　By him made perfect then in love.

Kelly's Hymns, Appendix no. 2, 1846

Cecil Frances Alexander. 1823–1895

MAKER OF HEAVEN AND EARTH

All things bright and beauteous,
 All creatures great and small,
All things wise and wondrous,
 The LORD GOD made them all.

Each little flower that opens,
 Each little bird that sings,
He made their glowing colours,
 He made their tiny wings.

The rich man in his castle,
 The poor man at his gate,
God made them, high or lowly,
 And ordered their estate.

The purple-headed mountain,
 The river running by,
The sunset, and the morning,
 That brightens up the sky,

The cold wind in the winter,
 The pleasant summer sun,
The ripe fruits in the garden,
 He made them every one.

The tall trees in the greenwood,
 The meadows where we play,
The rushes by the water,
 We gather every day;—

He gave us eyes to see them,
 And lips that we might tell,
How great is GOD Almighty,
 Who has made all things well.

SUFFERED UNDER PONTIUS PILATE, WAS CRUCIFIED, DEAD, AND BURIED

There is a green hill far away,
　　Without a city wall,
Where the dear LORD was crucified,
　　Who died to save us all.

We may not know, we cannot tell
　　What pains He had to bear,
But we believe it was for us,
　　He hung and suffered there.

He died that we might be forgiven,
　　He died to make us good,
That we might go at last to heaven,
　　Saved by His precious Blood.

There was no other good enough
　　To pay the price of sin,
He only could unlock the gate
　　Of Heaven, and let us in.

O, dearly, dearly has He loved,
　　And we must love Him too,
And trust in His redeeming Blood,
　　And try His works to do.

THE RESURRECTION OF THE BODY

Within the churchyard, side by side,
　　Are many long low graves,
And some have stones set over them,
　　On some the green grass waves.

Full many a little Christian child,
 Woman and man, lies there,
And we pass by them every time
 When we go into prayer.

They cannot hear our footsteps come,
 They do not see us pass,
They cannot feel the bright warm sun
 That shines upon the grass.

They do not hear when the great bell
 Is ringing overhead;
They cannot rise and come to Church
 With us, for they are dead.

But we believe a Day shall come,
 When all the dead will rise,
When they who sleep down in the grave,
 Will ope again their eyes.

For CHRIST our LORD was buried once,
 He died and rose again,
He conquered death, He left the grave,
 And so will Christian men.

So when the friends we loved the best,
 Lie in their churchyard bed,
We must not cry too bitterly
 Over the happy dead.

Because for our dear SAVIOUR'S sake
 Our sins are all forgiven,
And Christians only fall asleep
 To wake again in Heaven.

Hymns for Little Children, 1848

PASSION WEEK

"Touched with a feeling of our infirmities."

When wounded sore the stricken soul
    Lies bleeding and unbound,
One only hand—a pierced hand
    Can salve the sinner's wound.

When sorrow swells the laden breast,
    And tears of anguish flow,
One only heart—a broken heart
    Can feel the sinner's woe.

When penitence has wept in vain
    Over some foul dark spot,
One only stream, a stream of blood
    Can wash away the blot.

'Tis JESUS' blood that washes white,
    His hand that brings relief,
His heart that's touch'd with all our joys,
    And feeleth for our grief.

Lift up thy bleeding hand, O LORD,
    Unseal that cleansing tide,
We have no shelter from our sin,
    But in Thy wounded side.

THE CIRCUMCISION

JESUS, on Thine eighth day led,
Even then the Lamb that bled,
Circumcised that we might see
A redeeming infancy:

8

By those drops, the first red rains
Bursting from Thy bleeding veins,
Grant to us for Thy dear merit,
Circumcision of the spirit.

JESUS, on Thine eighth day hasting,
To Thy sorrow's bitter tasting;
Not one golden moment's loss
From Thy cradle to Thy cross;
Not one hour of daylight sun,
Wasted till Thy work was done;
JESUS, in this changeful clime
Teach us to redeem the time.

By the bitter woe, Thy cup,
On Thine eighth day filling up;
By the blood the sharp knife under;
By Thy saving name of wonder;
JESUS, grant us old and young,
Patience when the heart is wrung,
Giving all that GOD may claim,
Wearing well Thy worthy Name.

Hymns Descriptive and Devotional for the Use of Schools, 1858

ST. MARK THE EVANGELIST

"The face of a lion on the right side."

From out the cloud of amber light,
Borne on the whirlwind from the north,
Four living creatures winged and bright
Before the Prophet's eye came forth.

The voice of GOD was in the Four
Beneath that awful crystal mist,
And every wondrous form they wore
Foreshadowed an Evangelist.

The lion-faced, he told abroad
The strength of love, and strength of faith;
He showed the Almighty SON of GOD,
The Man Divine Who won by death.

O Lion of the Royal Tribe,
Strong SON of GOD, and strong to save,
All power and honour we ascribe
To Thee Who only makest brave.

For strength to love, for will to speak,
For fiery crowns by Martyrs won,
For suffering patience, strong and meek,
We praise Thee LORD, and Thee alone.

Hymns Ancient and Modern, 1875

Frederick William Faber. 1814–1863

THE AGONY

My God! My God! and can it be
That I should sin so lightly now,
And think no more of evil thoughts,
Than of the wind that waves the bough?

I sin, and heaven and earth go round,
As if no dreadful deed were done,
As if God's Blood had never flowed
To hinder sin, or to atone.

I walk the earth with lightsome step,
Smile at the sunshine, breathe the air,
Do my own will, nor ever heed
Gethsemane and Thy long prayer.

Shall it be always thus, O Lord?
Wilt Thou not work this hour in me
The grace Thy Passion merited,
Hatred of self and love of Thee?

O by the pains of Thy pure love,
Grant me the gift of holy fear;
And give me of Thy Bloody Sweat
To wash my guilty conscience clear!

Ever when tempted, make me see,
Beneath the olive's moon-pierced shade,
My God, alone, outstretched, and bruised,
And bleeding, on the earth He made.

And make me feel it was my sin,
As though no other sins there were,
That was to Him who bears the world
A load that He could scarcely bear!

Jesus and Mary, 1852

COMMUNION

O happy Flowers! O happy Flowers!
How quietly for hours and hours,
In dead of night, in cheerful day,
Close to my own dear Lord you stay,
Until you gently fade away!
O happy Flowers, what would I give
In your sweet place all day to live,
And then to die, my service o'er,
Softly as you do, at His door.

O happy Lights! O happy Lights!
Watching my Jesus livelong nights,
How close you cluster round His throne,
Dying so meekly one by one,
As each its faithful watch has done.

Could I with you but take my turn,
And burn with love of Him, and burn
Till love had wasted me, like you—
Sweet lights! what better could I do?

O happy Pyx! O happy Pyx!
Where Jesus doth His dwelling fix;
O little palace, dear and bright,
Where He, who is the world's true light,
Spends all the day, and stays all night!
Ah! if my heart could only be
A little home for Him like thee,
Such fires my happy soul would move,
I could not help but die of love!

O Pyx, and Lights, and Flowers! but I
Through envy of you will not die;
Nay, happy things! what will you do,
For I am better off than you,
The whole day long, the whole night through!
For Jesus gives Himself to me,
So sweetly and so utterly,
By rights long since I should have died
For love of Jesus Crucified.

My happy soul! My happy Soul!
How shall I then my love control?
O sweet Communion! Feast of bliss!
When the dear Host my tongue doth kiss,
What happiness is like to this?
O heaven, I think, must be alway
Quite like a First Communion Day;
With love so sweet and joy so strange,—
Only that heaven will never change!

Oratory Hymns, 1854

Charlotte Elliott. 1789–1871

John vi. 37

Just as I am—without one plea,
But that thy blood was shed for me,
And that thou bid'st me come to thee,
  O Lamb of God, I come!

Just as I am—and waiting not
To rid my soul of one dark blot,
To thee, whose blood can cleanse each spot,
  O Lamb of God, I come!

Just as I am—though tossed about
With many a conflict—many a doubt,
"Fightings and fears within, without,"
  O Lamb of God, I come!

Just as I am—poor, wretched, blind;
Sight, riches, healing of the mind,
Yea, all I need, in thee to find,
  O Lamb of God, I come!

Just as I am—thou wilt receive,
Wilt welcome, pardon, cleanse, relieve:
Because thy promise I believe,
  O Lamb of God, I come!

Just as I am—thy love unknown
Has broken every barrier down,
Now, to be thine, yea, thine alone,
  O Lamb of God, I come!

Invalid's Hymn Book, edition of 1854

Jemima Luke. 1813–1906

THE CHILD'S DESIRE

I think when I read that sweet story of old,
  When Jesus was here among men,
How he call'd little children, as lambs to his fold,
  I should like to have been with them then.
I wish that his hands had been placed on my head,
  That his arm had been thrown around me,
And that I might have seen his kind look when he said,
  'Let the little ones come unto me.'

Yet still to his footstool in prayer I may go,
  And ask for a share in his love;
And if I now earnestly seek him below,
  I shall see him and hear him above,—
In that beautiful place he is gone to prepare
  For all who are washed and forgiven;
And many dear children are gathering there,
  'For of such is the kingdom of heaven.'

But thousands and thousands who wander and fall,
  Never heard of that heavenly home,—
I should like them to know there is room for them all,
  And that Jesus has bid them to come.
I long for the joy of that glorious time,
  The sweetest, and brightest, and best,
When the dear little children of every clime
  Shall crowd to his arms and be blest.

Religious Tracts in Verse, 1856

John Hampton Gurney. 1802–1862

FIRST FRUITS

Fair waved the golden corn,
In Canaan's pleasant land,
When full of joy, some shining morn,
Went forth a reaper band.

To God, so good and great,
Their cheerful thanks they pour;
Then carry to his temple gate
The choicest of their store.

For thus the holy word
Spoken by Moses, ran—
"The first ripe ears are for the Lord,
The rest He gives to man."

May we, like Israel, give
Our earliest fruits to thee;
And pray that long as we shall live,
We may thy children be.

In wisdom let us grow,
As years and strength are given;
That we may serve thee here below,
And join thy saints in Heaven.

Select Hymns for Sunday Schools, 1857

James Drummond Burns. 1823–1864

Song of Solomon, i. 8

Not always, Lord, in pastures green
    The sheep at noon Thou feedest,
        Where in the shade they lie
        Within Thy watchful eye;
Not always under skies serene
    The white-fleeced flock Thou leadest.

On rugged ways, with bleeding feet,
    They leave their painful traces;
        Through deserts drear they go,
        Where wounding briars grow,
And through dark valleys, where they meet
    No quiet resting-places.

Not always by the waters still,
    Or lonely wells palm-hidden,
        Do they find happy rest,
        And, in Thy presence blest,
Delight themselves, and drink their fill
    Of pleasures unforbidden.

Their track is worn on Sorrow's shore,
    Where windy storms beat ever,—
        Their troubled course they keep,
        Where deep calls unto deep;
So going till they hear the roar
    Of the deep-flowing river.

But wheresoe'er their steps may be,
    So Thou their path be guiding,
        O be their portion mine!—

Show me the secret sign,
That I may trace their way to Thee,
And there find rest abiding.

Slowly they gather to the fold
Upon Thy holy mountain,—
There, resting round Thy feet,
They dread no storm nor heat,
And slake their thirst where Thou hast rolled
The stone from Life's full fountain.

The Vision of Prophecy, 1854

THE CHILD SAMUEL

Hushed was the evening hymn,
The temple courts were dark;
The lamp was burning dim
Before the sacred Ark,
When suddenly a voice divine
Rang through the silence of the shrine.

The old man, meek and mild,
The priest of Israel, slept;
His watch the temple child,
The little Levite, kept;
And what from Eli's sense was sealed,
The Lord to Hannah's son revealed.

O give me Samuel's ear,
The open ear, O Lord,
Alive and quick to hear
Each whisper of Thy word;
Like him to answer at Thy call,
And to obey Thee first of all.

O give me Samuel's heart,
A lowly heart that waits,
Where in Thy house Thou art,
Or watches at Thy gates;
By day and night, a heart that still
Moves at the breathing of Thy will.

O give me Samuel's mind,
A sweet unmurmuring faith,
Obedient and resigned
To Thee in life and death:
That I may read, with child-like eyes,
Truths that are hidden from the wise.

JACOB'S DREAM

He slept beneath the desert skies,
His pillar was the desert stone,
Yet heavenly visions blessed his eyes,
And cheered his spirit sad and lone.
He saw the stair of light let down,
Whose shining steps the angels trod,
And called the desert where it shone
The gate of heaven,—the house of God.

Thy sleepless eye, O God, still keeps
Its watch o'er every covenant heir;
And angels down that ladder's steps
From Thee to me a blessing bear.
Through Christ to Thee ascends my prayer,
Through Christ on me is grace bestowed;
Each place becomes, when Christ is there,
The gate of heaven,—the house of God.

In dungeons dark, in dwellings mean,
Where suffering saints have bent the knee,
That mystic ladder has been seen,
And angels come with gifts from Thee.

This night may I the vision see,
My spirit climb that radiant road;
This night my quiet chamber be
The gate of heaven,—the house of God.

The Evening Hymn, 1857

John Samuel Bewlay Monsell. 1811–1875

The foxes have holes, and the birds of the air have nests; but the Son of man hath not where to lay his head. Matt. vii. 20

Birds have their quiet nest,
Foxes their holes, and man his peaceful bed;
All creatures have their rest,—
But Jesus had not where to lay his head.

Winds have their hour of calm,
And waves, to slumber on the voiceless deep;
Eve hath its breath of balm
To hush all senses, and all sounds to sleep:

The wild deer hath his lair,
The homeward flocks the shelter of their shed;
All have their rest from care,—
But Jesus had not where to lay his head.

And yet He came to give
The weary and the heavy-laden rest;
To bid the sinner live,
And soothe our griefs to slumber on his breast.

What then am I, my God,
Permitted thus the paths of peace to tread?
Peace, purchas'd by the blood
Of Him who had not where to lay his head!

I, who once made Him grieve;
I, who once bid His gentle spirit mourn;
 Whose hand essay'd to weave
For His meek brow the cruel crown of thorn:—

 Oh why should I have peace,
Why? but for that unchang'd, undying love,
 Which would not, could not cease,
Until it made me heir of joys above.

 Yes! but for pardoning grace,
I feel I never should in glory see
 The brightness of that face,
That once was pale and agoniz'd for me!

 Let the birds seek their nest,
Foxes their holes, and man his peaceful bed;
 Come Saviour, in my breast
Deign to repose thine oft rejected head!

 Come! give me rest, and take
The only rest on earth thou lov'st,—within
 A heart, that for thy sake
Lies bleeding, broken, penitent for sin.

Hymns and Miscellaneous Poems, 1837

THE PENITENT

God be merciful to me a sinner.

Luke xviii. 13

Sinful, sighing to be blest,
 Bound, and longing to be free;
Weary, waiting for my rest,
 'God, be merciful to me!'

Holiness! I've none to plead,
　　Sinfulness, in all, I see;
I can only bring my need,
　　'God, be merciful to me!'

Broken heart, and downcast eyes,
　　Dare not lift themselves to Thee;
Yet Thou canst interpret sighs,
　　'God, be merciful to me!'

From this sinful heart of mine,
　　To thy bosom I would flee;
I am not mine own, but Thine,
　　'God be merciful to me!'

There is One, beside thy Throne,
　.　And my only hope and plea
Are in Him, and Him alone,
　　'God be merciful to me!'

He my cause will undertake,
　　My Interpreter will be;
He's my all—and for His sake,
　　'God, be merciful to me!'

Spiritual Songs, 1857

Edward Caswall. 1814–1878

O SOLA MAGNARUM URBIUM

Bethlehem! of noblest cities
　　None can once with thee compare;
Thou alone the Lord from Heaven
　　Didst for us Incarnate bear.

Fairer than the sun at morning
　　Was the star that told his birth;
To the lands their God announcing,
　　Hid beneath a form of earth.

By its lambent beauty guided
    See, the Eastern kings appear;
See them bend, their gifts to offer,—
    Gifts of incense, gold, and myrrh.

Offerings of mystic meaning!—
    Incense doth the God disclose;
Gold a royal child proclaimeth;
    Myrrh a future tomb foreshews.

Holy Jesu! in thy brightness
    To the Gentile world display'd!
With the Father, and the Spirit,
    Endless praise to Thee be paid.

                    Lyra Catholica, 1849

TO THE INFANT JESUS ASLEEP

    Sleep, Holy Babe,
    Upon Thy mother's breast!
Great Lord of earth and sea and sky,
How sweet it is to see Thee lie
    In such a place of rest!

    Sleep, Holy Babe!
    Thine Angels watch around;
All bending low, with folded wings,
Before th'Incarnate King of kings,
    In reverent awe profound!

    Sleep, Holy Babe!
    While I with Mary gaze
In joy upon that face awhile,
Upon the loving infant smile,
    Which there divinely plays.

Sleep, Holy Babe!
Ah, take Thy brief repose;
Too quickly will Thy slumbers break,
And Thou to lengthen'd pains awake,
That death alone shall close.

Then must those hands,
Which now so fair I see;
Those little pearly feet of Thine,
So soft, so delicately fine,
Be pierc'd and rent for me!

Then must that brow
Its thorny crown receive;
That cheek, more lovely than the rose,
Be drench'd with blood, and marr'd with blows,
That I thereby may live.

O Lady blest!
Sweet Virgin, hear my cry!
Forgive the wrong that I have done
To thee, in causing thy dear Son
Upon the Cross to die!

SWIFTNESS OF TIME

Days and moments quickly flying,
Blend the living with the dead;
Soon will you and I be lying
Each within our narrow bed.

Soon our souls, to God who gave them,
Will have sped their rapid flight;—
Able now by grace to save them,
O, that while we can we might!

Jesu, infinite Redeemer,
    Maker of this mighty frame!
Teach, O teach us to remember
    What we are, and whence we came;

Whence we came, and whither wending,
    Soon we must through darkness go,
To inherit bliss unending,
    Or eternity of woe.

A WARNING

As the tree falls,
    So must it lie;
As the man lives,
    So will he die;
As the man dies,
    Such must he be,
All through the days
    Of Eternity.

The Masque of Mary, 1858

William Whiting. 1825–1878

THOU RULEST THE RAGING OF THE SEA

Psalms. lx. xxix 10

O Thou Who bidd'st the ocean deep,
Its own appointed limits keep,
Thou, Who didst bind the restless wave,
Eternal FATHER, strong to save.
    O hear us when we cry to Thee
    For all in peril on the sea.

241

O Saviour, Whose almighty word
The wind and waves submissive heard,
Who walkedst on the foaming deep,
And calm amid the storm didst sleep;
> O hear us when we cry to Thee
> For all in peril on the sea.

O Sacred SPIRIT, Who didst brood
Upon the waters dark and rude,
Who bad'st their angry tumult cease,
And light diffused, and life, and peace.
> O hear us when we cry to Thee
> For all in peril on the sea.

O TRINITY of love and power,
Our brethren shield in danger's hour;
From rock and tempest them defend;
To safety's harbour them attend;
> And ever let there rise to Thee
> Glad hymns of praise from land and sea.

Hymns Ancient and Modern with Annotations by L. C. Biggs, 1867

James Edmeston. 1791–1867

CHILDREN'S PRAISE

Gentle angels, lowly bending,
> Love to hear when children sing,
With the artless voices blending,
> Join the praise and drop the wing.

If beneath some palmy cover
> Heathen babes encircled praise,
Would they not delighted hover,
> Grateful and adoring gaze.

242

While in simple hymns their voices,
    Swell to praise the Saviour's name,
Heaven itself the sound rejoices,
    Waking rapture to a flame.

ANGELS

Holy angels in their flight
    Traverse over earth and sky,
Acts of kindness their delight,
    Wing'd with mercy as they fly.

Though their form we cannot see,
    They attend and guard our way,
Till we join their company,
    In the fields of heavenly day.

Had we but an angel's wing,
    And an angel's heart of flame;
Oh! how sweetly would we ring
    Through the world the Saviour's name.

Yet methinks if I should die,
    And become a spirit too,
I perhaps like them might fly,
    And like them God's bidding do.

Infant Breathings, 1862

Christopher Wordsworth. 1807–1885

Hark the sound of holy voices, chanting at the crystal sea
Hallelujah! Hallelujah! Hallelujah! Lord to Thee.
Multitude, which none can number, like the stars, in glory
    stands
Cloth'd in white apparel, holding palms of Victory in their
    hands.

Patriarch, and holy Prophet, who prepar'd the Way of Christ,
King, Apostle, Saint, and Martyr, Confessor, Evangelist,
Saintly Maiden, godly Matron, Widows who have watch'd to
    prayer,
Join'd in holy concert singing to the Lord of all are there.

They have come from tribulation, and have wash'd their robes
    in Blood,
Wash'd them in the Blood of Jesus; tried they were, and firm
    they stood;
Mock'd, imprison'd, ston'd, tormented, sawn asunder, slain
    with sword,
They have conquer'd Death and Satan, by the might of Christ
    the Lord.

Marching with Thy Cross their banner, they have triumph'd,
    following
Thee the Captain of Salvation, Thee their Saviour and their
    King;
Gladly, Lord, with Thee they suffer'd; gladly, Lord, with
    Thee they died;
And by Death to Life immortal they were born and glorified.

Now they reign in heavenly glory, now they walk in golden
    light,
Now they drink, as from a river, holy bliss and infinite;
Love and Peace they taste for ever; and all Truth and Know-
    ledge see
In the beatific vision of the Blessed Trinity.

God of God, the One-begotten, Light of Light, Emmanuel,
In Whose Body join'd together all the Saints for ever dwell,
Pour upon us of Thy fulness, that we may for evermore
God the Father, God the Son, and God the Holy Ghost adore.

The Holy Year, 1863

William Chatterton Dix. 1837–1898

To Thee, O LORD, our hearts we raise
    In hymns of adoration;
To thee bring sacrifice of praise,
    With shouts of exultation.
Bright robes of gold the fields adorn,
    The hills with joy are ringing;
The valleys stand so thick with corn,
    That even they are singing.

And now, on this our festal day,
    Thy bounteous Hand confessing,
Upon Thine Altar, LORD, we lay
    The first-fruits of Thy blessing;
By Thee the souls of men are fed
    With gifts of grace supernal;
Thou Who dost give us daily bread,
    Give us the Bread Eternal.

We bear the burden of the day,
　　And often toil seems dreary,
But labour ends with sunset ray,
　　And rest is for the weary:
May we, the Angel reaping o'er,
　　Behold the tares rejected—
Ourselves GOD'S sheaves for evermore
　　To garners bright elected!

O, blessed is that land of GOD,
　　Where saints abide for ever;
Where golden fields spread fair and broad,
　　Where flows the crystal river.
The strains of all its holy throng
　　With ours to-day are blending;
Thrice blessed is that harvest song
　　Which never hath an ending.

St. Raphael's Hymns for the Service of the Church, 1864

Gerard Moultrie. 1829–1885

S. Mark,　+68. April 25

O God of armies, strong to save,
　　Whose glory led thine Israel
In safety through the Red Sea wave
　　When Egypt's chains of bondage fell,

Slow moved the cloud behind their host
　　With beams of GOD-impregnate light,
But frowning on the Egyptian coast
　　With shadows of the mid-day night.

Dark hangs the antitypal cloud,
 And red the wave must flow once more;
The Cross of Christ is in that shroud,
 The Blood of JESUS bathes the shore.

Lift up thy staff, O LORD, on high,
 And bid the Egyptian depths divide;
The Staff which grew on Calvary
 Shall rule o'er Death's rebellious tide.

Inspire the lion voice of Mark,
 And bid him dip his page therein;
To show the cloud no longer dark
 Whose Gospel-light dispels our sin.

PROCESSIONAL

S. Alban, Proto-Martyr of England, +*303. June 17*

Stand forth! stand forth, brave banner!
 The shield, the sword, and the battle:
For the LORD hath girded his loins for fight,
And the hosts of the faithful in armour bright,
 The shield, the sword and the battle,
Advance in serried and firm array
Full armed for the terrible battle day,
 The shield, the sword, and the battle.

The battle is of confuséd noise,
 The shield, the sword, and the battle,
The shout of the captains, which mingleth
With the neighing of that pale horse of death,
 The shield, the sword and the battle,
The banner unfurled from the Calvary Rood,
The garment of JESUS rolled in blood,
 The shield, the sword and the battle.

A hush falls over the plains of Death,
The shield, the sword, and the battle:
The hush of a host ere the shock of war,
The lull ere the thunder bursts afar,
The shield, the sword, and the battle:
But a sound goes up to the listening sky
Of souls which breathe but of victory,
The shield, the sword, and the battle.

Advance! advance, brave legions!
The shield, the sword, and the battle:
The vigil is o'er, the sentry past,
The fight for the faith is come at last,
The shield, the sword, and the battle.
Cast off the weight which encumbereth you,
And bear like a whirlwind, the battle through,
The shield, the sword, and the battle.

Your Lord who smote on the plains of death
The shield, the sword, and the battle,
Your captain who fought the fight so well
And tore the prize from the grasp of Hell,
The shield, the sword, and the battle,
He cometh! he cometh! behold his face!
In the van of his army he takes his place,
The shield, the sword, and the battle,
We fight for our own inheritance,
Stand forth, brave banner! Advance! Advance!
The shield, the sword, and the battle.

HARVEST HYMN

Heavenly FATHER, GOD alone,
Lo! before thy mercy-seat
We present thee of thine own,
Laying it before thy feet:
LORD of mercy and of grace,
Hear from Heaven thy dwelling-place.

Sheaves of wheat before thee lie,
    Bending low the heavy ear;
Bearded barley, grave ally
    With the fragile oat, is here:
        LORD of Mercy &c.

Clusters of the clinging vine
    Tenderly the corn-sheaves span,
With the Bread they join the Wine
    To make glad the heart of man:
        LORD of mercy &c.

Wedded cherries, ripe and red,
    Round the capitals are twined;
And the parsley hangs her head
    Filling up the space behind:
        LORD of mercy &c.

Pears from many an orchard smile,
All along the window-pane;
Rosy apples blush meanwhile
    On the rich and golden grain:
        LORD of mercy &c.

Joy is here; but joy will go
    Faster than these fruits decay,
And the life of man below
    Buds, and blooms, and fades away:
        LORD of mercy &c.

Summer days are past and gone,
    Autumn sunshine will not last,
And bright moments, one by one,
    Drop away into the past:
        LORD of mercy &c.

Thanks we give: and yet we pray
    In our Harvest Festival,
Teach us all to live to-day,
    For the Day which comes for all:
        LORD of mercy &c.

When the Master on that morn
With his harvesters shall come,
And shall gather in his corn,
    For the last great Harvest-home:
        LORD of mercy &c.

And the Angels reap the wheat,
    And bind up the ears of gold,
Yielding fruit about his feet
    Fifty and a hundredfold:
Bear these sheaves, O LORD of grace,
Into Heaven thy dwelling-place.

MIDNIGHT HYMN OF THE EASTERN CHURCH

Behold, the Bridegroom cometh in the middle of the night,
And blest is he whose loins are girt, whose lamp is burning
        bright;
But woe to that dull servant whom the Master shall surprise
With lamp untrimmed, unburning, and with slumber in his
        eyes.

Do thou, my soul, beware, beware lest thou in sleep sink down,
Lest thou be given o'er to death, and lose the golden crown;
But see that thou be sober, with watchful eye, and thus
Cry—"Holy, Holy, Holy GOD, have mercy upon us."

That day, the day of fear, shall come: my soul slack not thy
      toil,
But light thy lamp and feed it well, and make it bright with oil;
Who knowest not how soon may sound the cry at eventide,
"Behold, the Bridegroom comes! arise! go forth to meet the
      Bride."

Beware, my soul; beware, beware lest thou in slumber lie,
And, like the five, remain without, and knock, and vainly cry;
But watch, and bear thy lamp undimmed, and CHRIST shall
      gird thee on
His own bright wedding robe of Light—the glory of the SON.

*Hymns and Lyrics for the Seasons and Saints Days of the Church,
1867*

Sir Henry Williams Baker, Bart. 1821–1877

THE LORD IS MY SHEPHERD

The King of love my Shepherd is,
    Whose goodness faileth never;
I nothing lack if I am His,
    And He is mine for ever.

Where streams of living water flow
    My ransomed soul He leadeth,
And, where the verdant pastures grow,
    With food celestial feedeth.

Perverse and foolish oft I strayed,
    But yet in love He sought me,
And on His Shoulder gently laid,
    And home, rejoicing, brought me.

In death's dark vale I fear no ill
    With Thee, dear LORD, beside me;
Thy rod and staff my comfort still,
    Thy Cross before to guide me.

Thou spread'st a Table in my sight,
    Thy Unction grace bestoweth,
And oh! what transport of delight
    From Thy pure Chalice floweth.

And so through all the length of days
    Thy goodness faileth never;
Good Shepherd, may I sing Thy praise
    Within Thy house for ever.

Appendix to Hymns Ancient and Modern, 1868

Anonymous

HYMN FOR INCURABLES IN WORKHOUSES AND HOSPITALS

The days and weeks pass on, and yet I live:
No healing art can any respite give;
Weary and restless full of bitter grief,
No hope of succour, comfort or relief.
        Here I must lie
        Until I die.

I have no power to rise upon my bed,
Scarce on my pillow move my heavy head;
I am so feeble, so intensely weak,
Thought is an effort, and a pain to speak.
        Faintly I sigh,
        Lord, let me die.

At times my heart does long for some kind friend,
A sister or a child my bed to tend;
My heart will yearn with an unutter'd sigh,
For words of love and tender sympathy.
        Ah I must sigh
        Until I die.

I would not wish to murmur or complain,
I strive to trust these weary hours of pain
Are but as chastenings from a Father's hand
Fitting His child for that bright happy land;
        Thither I fly,
        Lord, when I die.

Yes, I *would* trust, but still hard thoughts will come
Wrestlings of spirit longing to go home;
The doubting question, wherefore this delay?
The faithless eye cast on the troubled way.
        Mournful I cry,
        When shall I die?

Thou poor worn spirit Jesus sees thy need;
He will not break, He says, the bruised reed:
He takes away from thee all earthly stay
To be Himself thy strength through all the way.
        He will be nigh
        Until thou die.

You long to spring again to active life,
Again to join the conflict and the strife,
You fain would aid another in distress,
And not live on in utter helplessness.
        Helplessly lie,
        Until you die.

It may not be. *Thy* work is to lie still,
The end of life is that our stubborn will
May be conformed to His: to do, to be,
As may seem best, O blessed Lord, to Thee;
    Tranquilly lie,
    Until thou die.

Did pain and grief and weariness depart,
Perchance the world again might have thy heart?
Hadst thou the tenderness for which you sigh,
Thou might seek less His perfect sympathy:
    Look less on high,
    For help to die.

Fear not, nor be afraid; there is no care,
No pain, no grief He does not with thee share;
In your affliction He afflicted is,
Your heavy burthens, lonely one, are His.
    On Him rely,
    Until you die.

Nor deem that useless is thy weary race,
No one is useless who fills up His place;
Thy lovely graces all around may shine
Like a pure light fed from a light Divine.
    Fed from on high,
    Until thou die.

In that last day when secret things are known,
Then will appear the work that Thou hast done;
Thy faith and love bright holy beams have shed,
Marking the path a Christian ought to tread.
    Patiently lie
    Ready to die.

Think too upon the mercies of thy lot,
You deem them small, but still forget them not;
Oh, think when resting on your humble bed,
The Saviour had not where to lay His head.
        And thankful lie
        Until you die.

Yet, think of mercies here! but most of those
Which may be yours when life's brief term shall close;
Of Jesus' dying love; of sin forgiven;
Of free renewing grace; and rest in heav'n.
        With Jesus nigh,
        There none shall die.

A broadsheet of about 1870

Henry Twells. 1823–1900

At even when the sun did set, they brought unto Him all that were diseased. St. Mark i. 32

At even ere the sun was set,
    The sick, O Lord, around Thee lay!
O, in what divers pains they met!
    O with what joy they went away!

Once more 'tis eventide, and we
    Oppressed with various ills draw near:
What if Thy form we cannot see?
    We know and feel that Thou art here.

O Saviour Christ, our woes dispel;
    For some are sick, and some are sad,
And some have never loved Thee well,
    And some have lost the love they had;

And some are pressed with worldly care;
    And some are tried with sinful doubt;
And some such grievous passions tear
    That only Thou canst cast them out;

And some have found the world is vain,
    Yet from the world they break not free;
And some have friends who give them pain,
    Yet have not sought a friend in Thee.

And none, O Lord, have perfect rest,
    For none are wholly free from sin;
And they who fain would serve Thee best
    Are conscious most of wrong within.

O Saviour Christ, Thou too art Man;
    Thou has been troubled, tempted, tried;
Thy kind but searching glance can scan
    The very wounds that shame would hide;

Thy touch has still its ancient power;
    No word from Thee can fruitless fall;
Hear, in this solemn evening hour,
    And in Thy mercy heal us all.

Church Hymns, 1871

Edward William Eddis

O King of peace, who standest
    Behind the jasper wall,
Where Joseph's fruitful branches
    In living clusters fall;

Thou comest from the mountain
    With myrrh and spices sweet;
And in the dews of morning
    We hear Thy blessed feet.

Jesu! Thy hidden presence
    The veil of flesh hath stirred;
And through the golden lattice
    Thy Bride Thy voice hath heard.

Come, Holy Lord, Thou feedest
    Among the lilies still;
The lowly ones shall blossom
    On God's eternal hill.

Thou strengthenest Thine anointed
    With manna from above;
Again with songs of promise
    We hear the Turtle-Dove.

Soon in Thine endless kingdom
    Thy glory shall be seen,
And Thou with stars of heaven
    Shalt crown Thy chosen Queen.

*   *   *

Still in Thy quiet garden,
    With angel-watchers blest,
Till earth's long night is over,
    Thine unseen armies rest.

And we Thy charge are keeping
    Before Thy holy hill:
O God, our hearts are heavy.
    Our eyes are holden still.

But in the hour of waking
    Thy sealed ones shall see
The fulness of the glory,
    Which now is hid with Thee.

9

And all at Thine appearing
   Their songs of joy shall raise,
Once more together, filling
   Thy house with glorious praise.

*   *   *

O Merciful High Priest! Thine almond rod
Hath lived and blossomed in the house of God.
Thine is the spotless ephod; Thine alone
The sevenfold lamps before the eternal throne.

Thine are the signet stones; the Oil Divine,
The purple robe, the golden bells, are Thine;
The fringe of heavenly blue, the gems of light,
The scarlet thread, the linen clean and white.

Thine incense burns with fourfold odours sweet
From Thine own hand before the mercy-seat:
Angel of God! Thy voice within the veil
Holds back the storms of earth; Thy prayers prevail.

Oh, glorify before Thy Father's throne
Thy wondrous paved work of sapphire stone:
Let all within Thy house in Thee rejoice,
And let the doors be moved at Thy voice.

Send forth Thy glorious Gospel; let the word
Of fear and hope through all the tribes be heard;
Comfort and guard us with Thy staff and rod,
And go before us to the Mount of God.

Still in the desert let Thy saints be fed
With Wine of gladness and with living Bread;
And guide us through the veil of earthly things,
In the safe covering of Thy seraphs' wings.

Hymns for the Use of the Churches, 1871

Godfrey Thring. 1823–1903

The Lord shall be Thine Everlasting Light Is. lx. 20

The radiant morn hath passed away,
And spent too soon her golden store,
The shadows of departing day
        Creep on once more.

Our life is but a fading dawn,
Its glorious noon how quickly past;
Lead us, O Christ, when all is gone
        Safe Home at last.

Oh! by Thy soul-inspiring grace
Uplift our hearts to realms on High;
Help us to look to that Bright Place
        Beyond the sky,

Where Light, and Life, and Joy, and Peace,
In undivided empire reign,
And thronging angels never cease
        Their deathless strain;

Where saints are clothed in spotless white,
And evening shadows never fall,
Where Thou, Eternal Light of Light,
        Art Lord of all.

GOD'S BARN

In the time of harvest I will say to the reapers . . . Gather the wheat into my barn. Matt. xiii. 30

She is gone to the land whence the white reapers come,
　To gather the corn that is full in the ear,
And lay it in store till the last Harvest Home,
　When the Lord of the Harvest Himself shall appear.

Toil, trouble, and care had been sown in the field,
　And ripened its seed with the ripening grain;
The thorn and the thistle that grew side by side,
　Were watered alike by the dew and the rain.

The thorn and the thistle lie sodden and soiled,
　To be trod underfoot by the lone passer-by;
The grain that had grown on the same furrowed field,
　Is gathered and garnered by angels on High.

No memory now of the tears that are shed,
　The cares and the sorrows lie low in the sod,
The faith and the love and the works of a life,
　Are ripened and stored in the barn of her God.

May He Who's the One loving Father of all,
　Who watches o'er all with His tenderest care,
Send His angels from Heaven when our Harvest is ripe,
　And gather us in to be harvested there.

LENT

Let us therefore come boldly to the throne of grace, that we may obtain mercy, and find grace to help in time of need. Heb. iv. 16

Hast thou sinnèd, sin no more,
　Pardon ask, and pardon win,
Mercy sits at mercy's door,
　Boldly knock and enter in;

Boldly to the throne of grace,
 Weeping for the bitter past,
Go, though shame would hide its face,
 Go, and find a rest at last;

Christ, Who died the lost to save,
 Never turned His Face from pain,
They who meekly pardon crave,
 Never cry to Him in vain;

Christ Himself is calling, "Come,"
 Christ, Who lived and died for thee,
"Hasten, helpless sinner, home,
 Lay your weary load on Me."

Fear not, then, to lay it down
 Humbly at your Saviour's Feet,
Through the Cross to win the Crown,
 Is a task for Angels meet;

Stand not still to count the cost,
 Hasten while 'tis yet today,
Time, too precious to be lost,
 Brooks not doubt, away—away.

Yes! away ere yet the light
 Darkens in the western sky,
And the brooding clouds of night
 Hover o'er your sunken eye;

Yes! in this thy sorest need,
 Knock in faith at mercy's door;
Go, and there for pardon plead,
 Go, for grace to sin no more.

Hymns and Sacred Lyrics, 1874

Samuel John Stone. 1839–1900

THE FORGIVENESS OF SINS

Weary of earth, and laden with my sin;
I look at heaven and long to enter in;
But there no evil thing may find a home;
And yet I hear a voice that bids me 'Come.'

So vile I am, how dare I hope to stand
In the pure glory of that holy land?
Before the whiteness of that throne appear?
Yet there are Hands stretched out to draw me near.

The while I fain would tread the heavenly way,
Evil is ever with me day by day;
Yet on mine ears the gracious tidings fall,
'Repent, confess, thou shalt be loosed from all.'

It is the voice of Jesus that I hear,
His are the hands stretched out to draw me near,
And His the Blood that can for all atone,
And set me faultless there before the throne.

'Twas He who found me on the deathly wild,
And made me heir of heaven, the Father's child,
And day by day, whereby my soul may live,
Gives me His grace of pardon, and will give.

O great Absolver! grant my soul may wear
The lowliest garb of penitence and prayer,
That in the Father's courts my glorious dress
May be the garment of Thy righteousness.

Yea, Thou wilt answer for me, righteous Lord;
Thine all the merits, mine the great reward;
Thine the sharp thorns, and mine the golden crown;
Mine the life won, and Thine the life laid down!

Naught can I bring, dear Lord, for all I owe;
Yet let my full heart what it can bestow;
Like Mary's gift let my devotion prove,
Forgiven greatly, how I greatly love.

Hymns, 1887

D.M.

Two little hands I have,
    To clap when I am glad;
Two little eyes that fill with tears,
    When I am hurt or sad.

A little voice I have,
    That speaks or softly sings;
Two little feet that walk or run—
    Such tiny, restless things.

A home and friends I have,
    And dress and daily food.
O may I never once forget
    'Tis God who is so good.

O may He teach my heart
    To hate what is not true,
And guide my helpless, little hands
    In everything they do.

O may He keep my feet
    Within His holy ways,
And help my voice each day to sing
    A thankful song of praise.

Hymns for the Little Ones, 1892

J. H. Ernest While

Dedicated to all those, our Brothers, who toil in the Deep Places of the Earth.

Father in Heaven, by Whose Almighty Word
The vast foundations of the earth are stirr'd;
Saviour of sinners, in Thy Love Divine,
Guard and protect Thy children in the mine.

Dark are our ways, O Lord; in pity see
The souls who toil beneath the ground for Thee;
Deep in the fastnesses of earth we stand,
Keep us within the hollow of Thy Hand.

Be unto us, O Lord, our Guiding Lamp
From flood or vapour, flame, or after-damp;
Light o'er our pathway in Thy Mercy shine,
And shield us from the terrors of the mine.

God of all Love, Who changest not with years,
Comfort each mourner in this vale of tears;
No depth can keep us from Thy rest above,
No height shall part us from our Saviour's love.

Out of Thy bounteous store let Sovereign grace
Descend into earth's inmost, deepest place;
Pardon each sinful deed, or thought or ill,
Render our hearts submissive to Thy will.

Forth in Thy strength, O Lord, Thy children go,
Gladly to work the way which Thou shalt shew;
That in the mine, if there our call need be,
Its darkest path shall lead to Light—and Thee.

A broadsheet, 1908

Samuel Davies. 1723–1761

THE DIFFERENT STATES OF SINNERS AND SAINTS IN
THE WRECK OF NATURE

Isa. xxiv. 18–20

How great, how terrible that GOD,
Who shakes Creation with his Nod!
He frowns, and Earths' Foundations shake
And all the Wheels of Nature break.

Crush'd under Guilts' oppressive Weight
The Globe now totters to its Fate,
Trembles beneath its guilty Sons,
And for Deliv'rance loudly groans:

And see the glorious dreadful Day,
That takes th'enormous Load away!
See Ocean, Earth, all Nature's Frame
Sink in one universal Flame.

Where now, Oh where shall Sinners seek
For Shelter in the gen'ral wreck?
Shall falling Rocks be o'er them thrown?
See Rocks, like Snow, dissolving down.

In vain for Mercy now they cry;
In Lakes of liquid Fire they lie;
There on the flaming Billows tost,
For ever, Oh for ever lost!

But, Saints, undaunted and serene
Your Eyes shall view the dreadful Scene;
Your Saviour lives, tho' Worlds expire,
And Earth and Skies dissolve in Fire.

JESUS, the helpless Creature's Friend,
To Thee my All I dare commend:
Thou can'st preserve my feeble Soul,
When Lightnings blaze from Pole to Pole.

Written 1755, Hymns Adapted to Divine Worship collected by
Thomas Gibbons, 1769

Anonymous

CHRIST THE APPLE-TREE

The tree of life my soul hath seen,
Laden with fruit, and always green:
The trees of nature fruitless be,
Compar'd with Christ the apple-tree.

His beauty doth all things excel:
By faith I know, but ne'er can tell,
The glory which I now can see,
In Jesus Christ the apple-tree.

For happiness I long have sought,
And pleasure dearly I have bought:
I miss'd of all; but now I see
'Tis found in Christ the apple-tree.

I'm weary'd with my former toil,
Here I will sit and rest a while:
Under the shadow I will be,
Of Jesus Christ the apple-tree.

With great delight I'll make my stay,
There's none shall fright my soul away:
Among the sons of men I see
There's none like Christ the apple-tree.

I'll sit and eat this fruit divine,
It cheers my heart like spirit'al wine;
And now this fruit is sweet to me,
That grows on Christ the apple-tree.

This fruit doth make my soul to thrive,
It keeps my dying faith alive;
Which makes my soul in haste to be
With Jesus Christ the apple-tree.

*Published 1761 in an English magazine; incorporated in Divine
Hymns, edited by Joshua Smith, 1804*

POOR WAYFARING STRANGER

I'm just a poor wayfaring stranger,
A-trav'ling through this world of woe,
But there's no sickness, toil or danger
In that bright land to which I go.
    I'm going there to see my father,
    I'm going there no more to roam,
    I'm just a-going over Jordan,
    I'm just a-going over home.

I'm just a poor wayfaring stranger,
A-trav'ling through this world of woe,
But there's no sickness, toil or danger
In that bright land to which I go.
    I'm going there to see my mother,
    She said she'd meet me when I come;
    I'm just a-going over Jordan,
    I'm just a-going over home.

Post-Revolutionary camp-meeting hymn

THE FAREWELL

Farewell my brethren in the Lord,
    The gospel sounds a jubilee;
My stamm'ring tongue shall sound aloud,
    From land to land, from sea to sea:
And as I preach from place to place,
I'll trust alone in God's free grace.

Farewell, in bonds and union dear;
    Like strings you twine about my heart:
I humbly beg your earnest pray'r,
    Till we shall meet, no more to part—
Till we shall meet in worlds above,
Encircled in eternal love.

Farewell my earthly friends below,
    Though all so kind and dear to me;
My Jesus calls, and I must go
    To sound the gospel jubilee—
To sound the joys, and bear the news
To Gentile worlds and royal Jews.

Farewell young people, one and all;
    While God shall grant me breath to breathe,
I'll pray to the Eternal All,
    That your dear souls in Christ may live—
That your dear souls prepar'd may be
To reign in bliss eternally!

Farewell to all below the sun;
    And, as I pass in tears below,
The path is straight my feet shall run:
    And God will keep me as I go;
And God will keep me in his hand,
And bring me to the promis'd land.

Farewell, farewell! I look above;
Jesus, my friend, to thee I call:
My joy, my crown, my only love,
   My safeguard here, my heav'nly all;
My theme to preach, my song to sing,
My only joy till death—Amen.

CHRIST'S INVITATION TO HIS SPOUSE

Arise, my dear love, and undefil'd dove,
I hear my dear Jesus to say,
The winter is past, the spring's come at last,
   My love, my dove, come away.

The earth that is green, is fair to be seen,
The little birds chirping, do say,
That they do rejoice in each other's voice,
   My love, my dove, come away.

All smiling in love the young turtle dove,
The flower appearing in May,
I'll speak forth the praise of the ancient of days,
   My love, my dove, come away.

Come away from the world's cares, those troublesome
      snares,
That follow you night and by day,
That you may be free from the troubles that be,
   My love, my dove, come away.

Come away from all fear, that troubles you here,
Come into my arms, he doth say,
That you may be clear from the troubles you fear,
   My love, my dove, come away.

Come away from all pride, from that raging tide,
That makes you fall out by the way—
Come learn to be meek, and your Jesus to seek,
My love, my dove, come away.

As t'you that are old, and whose hearts are grown
cold,
Your Jesus inviting doth say,
That he's heard your cries in the north countries,
My love, my dove, come away.

As to you that are young, your hearts they are strong,
Your Jesus invites you away
From Antichrist's charms, to Jesus' kind arms,
My love, my dove, come away.

And as to the youth that have known the truth,
Whose hearts they have led them astray,
Come hear to his voice and your hearts shall rejoice,
My love, my dove, come away.

My dear children all, come hear to my call,
While I stand knocking and say,
My head's wet with dew, my children, for you,
My love, my dove, come away.

My fatlings are kill'd, my table is fill'd,
My maidens attending do say—
There's wine on the lees, as much as you please,
My love, my dove, come away.

Come travel the road that leads you to God,
For it is a bright shining way;
Come run up and down, my errands upon,
My love, my dove, come away.

Divine Hymns, 1804

THE SHAKERS

Anonymous

When we assemble here to worship God,
To sing his praises and to hear his word
   We will walk softly.

With purity of heart; and with clean hands,
Our souls are free, we're free from Satan's bands
   We will walk softly.

While we are passing thro' the sacred door,
Into the fold where Christ has gone before,
   We will walk softly.

We'll worship and bow down we will rejoice
And when we hear the shepherd's gentle voice
   We will walk softly.

MS. hymnal

I will bow and be simple
I will bow and be free
I will bow and be humble
Yea bow like the willow-tree
I will bow this is the token
I will wear the easy yoke
I will bow and be broken
Yea I'll fall upon the rock.

North family, New Lebanon (?) Shakers

THE HUMBLE HEART

Whence comes this bright celestial light,
What cause produces this,
A heaven opens to my sight,
Bright scenes of joy and bliss.
O Lord Jehovah art Thou here,
This light proclaims Thou art,
I am indeed, I'm always near
Unto the humble heart.

The proud and lofty I despise,
And bless the meek and low,
I hear the humble soul that cries,
And comfort I bestow.
Of all the trees among the wood
I've chose one little vine,
The meek and low are nigh to me,
The humble heart is mine.

Tall cedars fall before the wind,
The tempest breaks the oak,
Will slender vines will bow & bend
And rise beneath the stroke.
I've chosen me one pleasant grove
And set my lovely vine,
Here in my vineyard I will rove,
The humble heart is mine.

Of all the fowls that beat the air
I've chose one little dove,
I've made her spotless white & fair,
The object of my love.
Her feathers are like purest gold,
With glory she does shine,
She is a beauty to behold,
Her humble heart is mine.

Of all the kinds that range at large,
I've chose one little flock,
And those I make my lovely charge,
Before them I will walk.
Their constant shepherd I will be,
And all their ways refine,
And they shall serve & rev'rence me,
The humble heart is mine.

Of all the sects that fill the land
One little band I've chose,
And led them forth by my right hand
And plac'd my love on those.
The lovely object of my love,
Around my heart shall twine
My flock, my vineyard & my dove,
The humble heart is mine.

The George DeWitt MS. hymnal, 1822

William Augustus Muhlenberg. 1796–1877

Like Noah's weary dove,
　　That soared the earth around,
But not a resting place above
　　The cheerless waters found;

O cease, my wondering soul,
　　On restless wing to roam;
All the wide world, to either pole,
　　Has not for thee a home.

Behold the ark of God,
　　Behold the open door;
Hasten to gain that dear abode,
　　And rove, my soul, no more.

There, safe shalt thou abide,
 There, sweet shall be thy rest,
And every longing satisfied,
 With full salvation blest.

And when the waves of ire
 Again the earth shall fill,
The ark shall ride the sea of fire,
 Then rest on Sion's hill.

The Episcopal Hymn Book, 1826

Arthur Cleveland Coxe. 1818–1896

HYMN IN HOLY WEEK

Who is this, with garments gory,
 Triumphing from Bozrah's way,
This, that weareth robes of glory,
 Bright, with more than Vict'ry's ray;
Who is this unwearied comer
 From his journey's sultry length,
Travelling through Idume's summer,
 In the greatness of his strength!

Wherefore red in thine apparel,
 Like the conquerors of earth,
And arrayed like those who carol
 O'er the reeking vineyard's mirth.
Who art thou, the valleys seeking,
 Where our peaceful harvests wave!
I—in righteous anger speaking,
 I—the mighty One to save.

I—that of the raging heathen
    Trod the wine-press all alone,
Now in victor garlands wreathen,
    Coming to redeem Mine own.
I am He with sprinkled raiment,
    Glorious from My vengeance hour,
Ransoming with priceless payment,
    And delivering with power.

Hail, all hail, Thou LORD of Glory!
    Thee our Father—Thee we own!
Abram heard not of our story,
    Israel ne'er our name hath known;
But, Redeemer, Thou has sought us,
    Thou has heard Thy children's wail,
Thou with Thy dear blood has bought us,
    Hail, Thou mighty Victor, hail!

Christian Ballads and Poems, 1849

Lydia Sigourney. 1791–1865

THE DELUGE AND THE ARK

There was a noble ark,
Sailing o'er the waters dark
    And wide around;
Not one tall tree was seen,
Nor flow'r, nor leaf of green—
    All, all was drown'd!

Then a soft wing was spread,
And, o'er the billows dread,
    A meek dove flew;
But, on that shoreless tide,
No living thing she spied,
    To cheer her view.

So to the ark she fled,
With weary, drooping head,
    To seek for rest.
Christ is thine ark, my friend,
For thee he now doth send,
    Fly to his breast!

Select Hymns for Sunday Schools, 1857

Julia Ward Howe. 1819–1910

BATTLE-HYMN OF THE REPUBLIC

Mine eyes have seen the glory of the coming of the Lord:
He is trampling out the vintage where the grapes of wrath are
        stored;
He hath loosed the fateful lightning of his terrible swift sword:
    His truth is marching on.

I have seen Him in the watch-fires of a hundred circling camps;
They have builded Him an altar in the evening dews and
        damps;
I can read His righteous sentence by the dim and flaring lamps.
    His day is marching on.

I have read a fiery gospel, writ in burnished rows of steel:
"As ye deal with my contemners, so with you my grace shall
        deal;
Let the Hero, born of woman, crush the serpent with his heel,
    Since God is marching on."

He has sounded forth the trumpet that shall never call retreat;
He is sifting out the hearts of men before his judgement-seat:
Oh! be swift, my soul, to answer Him! be jubilant, my feet!
    Our God is marching on.

In the beauty of the lilies Christ was born across the sea,
With a glory in his bosom that transfigures you and me:
As he died to make men holy, let us die to make men free,
    While God is marching on.

Later Lyrics, 1866

Phillips Brooks. 1835–1893

O little town of Bethlehem,
    How still we see thee lie!
Above thy deep and dreamless sleep
    The silent stars go by.
Yet in thy dark streets shineth
    The everlasting Light;
The hopes and fears of all the years
    Are met in thee to-night.

O morning stars, together
    Proclaim the holy birth!
And praises sing to God the King,
    And peace to men on earth.
For Christ is born of Mary
    And gathered all above,
While mortals sleep the angels keep
    Their watch of wondering love.

How silently, how silently,
    The wondrous gift is given!
So God imparts to human hearts
    The blessings of His heaven.
No ear may hear his coming;
    But in this world of sin,
Where meek souls will receive Him still,
    The dear Christ enters in.

Where children pure and happy
    Pray to the blessed Child,
Where misery cries out to Thee,
    Son of the Mother mild.
Where charity stands watching,
    And Faith holds wide the door,
The dark night wakes, the glory breaks,
    And Christmas comes once more.

O holy Child of Bethlehem,
    Descend to us we pray!
Cast out our sin and enter in;
    Be born in us to-day.
We hear the Christmas angels
    The great glad tidings tell;
O come to us, abide with us,
    Our Lord Emmanuel!

Written for his Sunday School, 1868

Edmund Hamilton Sears. 1810–1876

CHRISTMAS CAROLS

It came upon the midnight clear,
    That glorious song of old,
From angels bending near the earth
    To touch their harps of gold;
"Peace on the earth, good-will to men
    From heaven's all-gracious King"—
The world in solemn stillness lay
    To hear the angels sing.

Still through the cloven skies they come
    With peaceful wings unfurled,
And still their heavenly music floats
    O'er all the weary world;

Above its sad and lowly plains
    They bend on hovering wing,
And ever o'er its Babel-sounds
    The blessed angels sing.

But with the woes of sin and strife
    The world has suffered long;
Beneath the angel-strain have rolled
    Two thousand years of wrong;
And man, at war with man, hears not
    The love-song which they bring;—
Oh hush the noise, ye men of strife,
    And hear the angels sing!

And ye, beneath life's crushing load,
    Whose forms are bending low,
Who toil along the climbing way
    With painful steps and slow,
Look now! for glad and golden hours
    Come swiftly on the wing;—
Oh rest beside the weary road,
    And hear the angels sing!

For lo! the days are hastening on,
    By prophet-bards foretold,
When with the ever circling years
    Comes round the age of gold;
When Peace shall over all the earth
    Its ancient splendors fling,
And the whole world give back the song
    Which now the angels sing.

Sermons and Songs of the Christian Life, 1875

TEMPERANCE HYMNS

Anonymous

APPEAL

Arise my tenderest thoughts arise,
To torrents melt my streaming eyes;
And thou, my heart, with anguish beat,
While drunkards perish in the street.

See human nature sunk in shame;
See scandal poured on Jesu's name;
The laws of God are trampled on;
The world abus'd, and souls undone.

See the short course of vain delight
Closing in everlasting night;
In flames that no abatement know,
Though briny tears forever flow.

My God, I shudder at the scene;
My bowels yearn o'er dying men;
And fain my pity would reclaim,
And snatch the drunkard from the flame.

Lend, lend thy aid, O God of truth,
To save the aged and the youth;
Thine own all-saving arm employ,
And turn this grief to richest joy.

PERVERSION OF THE DIVINE GOODNESS

God gave the gift to man;
　　But man with fatal skill,
Insensate form'd the plan
　　To change the good for ill:
The poison tortur'd from the cane,
Like Sampson hath its thousands slain.

God gave the golden grain
　　To hungry man for food;
But querulous and vain,
　　He spurn'd the proffer'd good:
And Egypt's slothful sons, athirst,
Drew forth the drowsy beverage first.

God gave the clustering vine;
　　Ingenious man perverse,
Exchang'd the boon for wine
　　And wrought Canaan's curse.
The patriarch, who had safely past
The deluge, was o'erwhelmed at last.

To earth the cup he hurled,
　　That holds an adder's sting;
And let us pledge the world
　　With nectar from the spring;
That hence, like Rechab's ancient line,
Though prophets urge, we drink no wine.

New London Temperance Hymn Book, 1839

Horatius Bonar. 1808–1889

THY WAY, NOT MINE

Thy way, not mine, O Lord,
    However dark it be!
Lead me by thine own hand,
    Choose out the path for me.

Smooth let it be or rough,
    It will be still the best,
Winding or straight, it matters not,
    It leads me to thy rest.

I dare not choose my lot:
    I would not, if I might;
Choose thou for me, my God,
    So shall I walk aright.

The kingdom that I seek
    Is thine; so let the way
That leads to it be thine,
    Else I must surely stray.

Take thou my cup, and it
    With joy or sorrow fill,
As best to thee may seem;
    Choose thou my good and ill.

Choose thou for me my friends,
    My sickness or my health,
Choose thou my cares for me,
    My poverty or wealth.

Not mine, not mine the choice,
    In things or great or small;
Be thou my guide, my strength,
    My wisdom, and my all.

A PILGRIM'S SONG

A few more years shall roll,
　　A few more seasons come;
And we shall be with those that rest,
　　Asleep within the tomb.
Then, O my Lord, prepare
　　My soul for that great day;
O wash me in thy precious blood,
　　And take my sins away.

A few more suns shall set
　　O'er these dark hills of time;
And we shall be where suns are not,
　　A far serener clime.
Then, O my Lord, prepare
　　My soul for that blest day;
O wash me in thy precious blood,
　　And take my sins away.

A few more storms shall beat
　　On this wild rocky shore;
And we shall be where tempests cease,
　　And surges swell no more.
Then, O my Lord, prepare
　　My soul for that calm day;
O wash me in thy precious blood,
　　And take my sins away.

A few more struggles here,
　　A few more partings o'er,
A few more toils, a few more tears,
　　And we shall weep no more.
Then, O my Lord, prepare
　　My soul for that blest day;
O wash me in thy precious blood,
　　And take my sins away.

A few more Sabbaths here
    Shall cheer us on our way;
And we shall reach the endless rest,
    The eternal Sabbath-day.
Then, O my Lord, prepare
    My soul for that sweet day;
O wash me in thy precious blood,
    And take my sins away.

'Tis but a little while
    And He shall come again,
Who died that we might live, who lives
    That we with Him may reign.
Then, O my Lord, prepare
    My soul for that glad day;
O wash me in thy precious blood,
    And take my sins away.

Hymns of Faith and Hope, First Series, 1857

THE GRAVES OF OCEAN

The sea gave up the dead which were in it.—Rev. xx. 13

Deep down beneath the unresting surge
    There is a peaceful tomb;
Storm raves above, calm reigns below;
Safe, safe from ocean's wreck and woe;
Safe from its tide's unceasing flow,
    The weary find a home.

Calm shelter from Time's vexing winds;
    Sure anchorage at last!
The blinding sea-drift blinds not here;
No breaker's boom the sleepers fear,
No angry typhoon hovers near—
    Their latest storm is past.

Done now with peril and with toil,
  They sleep the blessed sleep.
The last wild hurricane is o'er;
All silent now life's thunder-roar,
All quiet now the wreck-strewn shore;—
  'Tis *we*, not *they*, who weep.

Who dies in Christ the Lord dies well,
  Though on the lonely main;
As soft the pillow of the deep,
As tranquil the uncurtain'd sleep
As on the couch where fond ones weep;—
  And they shall rise again.

Not safer on the sea of glass
  Before the throne of God!
As sacred is that ocean-cave,
Where weeds instead of myrtles wave;
As near to God that unknown grave,
  As the dear churchyard's sod.

O'er the loved clay God sets his watch,
  The angels guard it well,
Till summon'd by the trumpet loud,
Like star emerging from the cloud,
Or blossom from its sheltering shroud,
  It leaves its ocean-cell.

The sea shall give them back, though death
  The well-known form destroy;
Nor rock, nor sand, nor foam can chain,
Nor mortal prison-house retain,
Each atom shall awake again,
  And rise with song and joy.

The cold sea's coldest, hardest depths
 Shall hear the trump of God,
Death's reign on sea and land is o'er,
God's treasured dust he must restore,
God's buried gems he holds no more,
 Beneath or wave or clod.

When the cold billow cover'd them,
 No solemn prayer was said;
Yet not the less their crown shall be
In the great morn of victory,
When, from their mortal fetters free,
 They leave their peaceful bed.

What though to speak the words of love
 No dear ones then could come.
Without a name upon their bier,
A brother's or a sister's tear,
Their heaven will be as bright and near
 As from their boyhood's home.

Star of the promised morning, rise!
 Star of the throbbing wave,
Ascend! and o'er the sable brine
With resurrection-splendour shine;
Burst through the clouds with beams divine,
 Mighty to shine and save.

O Morning Star! O risen Lord!
 Destroyer of the tomb!
Star of the living and the dead,
Lift up at length thy long-veil'd head,
O'er land and sea thy glories shed;—
 Light of the morning, come!

Into each tomb thy radiance pour,
    Let life, not death, prevail.
Make haste, great Conqueror, make haste!
Call up the dead of ages past,
Gather thy precious gems at last,
    From ocean's deepest vale.

Speak, mighty Life, and wake the dead!
    Like statue from the stone,
Like music from long broken strings,
Like gushings from deserted springs,
Like dew upon the dawn's soft wings,
    Rouse each beloved one!

Hymns of Faith and Hope, Second Series, 1861

HE MUST INCREASE, I MUST DECREASE

He must grow greater, I grow less and less:
    I like the mist which o'er the mountain flies,
And in the rising glory vanishes;
    He like the sun in yon fair morning skies;—
Amen, amen, I would not have it otherwise.

His name among the nations shall go forth,
    Above all names that earth has ever known;
A name for ages, name of matchless worth,
    Enduring when each other name is gone,
And this poor name of mine to dark oblivion thrown.

His story over earth shall yet be told,
    A story for the universe to hear,—
A wondrous story, which shall ne'er grow old,
    But fresher yet shall grow, and yet more dear,
When my brief tale is told of sin and want and fear.

His love, the more than sunshine for all things
    And beings, or above or here below,
Shall fly abroad on everlasting wings,
    Gladdening all space and time with its swift flow,
Till this cold love of mine be lost in its bright glow.

His voice, that fills the heaven of heavens with bliss,—
    The more than music of each listening ear,
Itself the melody of melodies,—
    Swells out o'er space, entrancing sphere on sphere,
Till this frail voice of mine is hushed with love and fear.

His throne, before whose majesty so few
    On earth now bow, shall be of thrones the throne,
Its splendour ever bright and ever new;
    While on His head there rests the eternal crown,
When from each brow of earth the glittering gold has
    gone.

Hymns of the Nativity, 1879

Anonymous

THE SPIRITUAL RAILWAY

The line to Heaven by Christ was made,
With Heavenly truths the rails are laid,
From earth to Heaven the line extends,
To life eternal, where it ends.

Repentance is the station then,
Where passengers are taken in;
No fee for them is there to pay
For Jesus is himself the way.

The bible is the engineer,
It points the way to Heaven so clear,
Through tunnels dark and dreary here,
It does the way to glory steer.

God's love the fire, his truth the steam,
Which drives the engine and the train,
All you who would to glory ride,
Must come to Christ, in him abide.

In first, and second, and third class,
Repentance, faith and holiness:
You must the way to Glory gain;
Or you with Christ can never reign.

Come then poor Sinner, now's the time,
At any Station on the Line.
If you repent and turn from sin,
The train will stop and take you in.

The Illustrated Testament, about 1870

Richard Weaver. 1827–1896

Saw ye my Saviour, saw ye my Saviour,
Saw ye my Saviour and God?
   He died on Calvary,
   To atone for you and me,
And to purchase our pardon with blood.

> *I do believe it—I do believe it,*
> *I am saved through the blood of the Lamb:*
> *My happy soul is free—for the Lord hath pardoned*
>   *me,*
> *Hallelujah to Jesus the Lamb.*

He was afflicted—He was afflicted,
On Him lay the sins of us all;
   As a Lamb to slaughter led
   So the lowly Saviour bled,
To redeem from the curse of the fall.

He was extended, He was extended,
Shamefully nailed to the cross,
   He bowed his head and died!
   Thus my Lord was crucified,
To atone for a world that was lost.

Jesus hung bleeding, Jesus hung bleeding,
Three dreadful hours in pain,
   The sun refused to shine,
   While his Majesty Divine,
Was derided, insulted, and slain.

There as my Surety, there as my Surety,
Jesus, my Lord, I do see,
   On Him my sins were laid,
   And for me the debt He paid,
When He groaned and expired on the tree.

Now interceding, now interceding,
Pleading that sinners might live,
   Saying, "Father, I have died,
   See my wounded hands and side!
I've redeemed them, I pray Thee forgive."

"I will forgive them, I will forgive them,
If they repent and believe;
   Let them turn unto me,
   And depend alone on Thee,
And salvation they freely shall have."

He has arisen! He has arisen!
A conqueror o'er death and the grave;
   Since Jesus rose, who died,
   God declares I'm justified,
And that Jesus is mighty to save.

He has ascended! He has ascended!
And now sits enthroned in the sky;
But He'll soon come to bear
All His ransomed people there,
And they'll reign kings with Jesus on high.

*Richard Weaver's Hymn-Book 1861; refrain and verses 2 and the
last two from Ned Wright's Hymnbook, 1870*

Edward Wright

Hark! hark! hear the glad tidings; soon, soon Jesus will come,
Robed, robed in honour and glory, to gather His ransomed
   ones home.
Yes, yes, oh yes! to gather His ransomed ones home.

Joy, joy, sound it more loudly: sing, sing glory to God;
Soon, soon Jesus is coming; publish the tidings abroad;
Yes, yes, oh yes! publish the tidings abroad.

Bright, bright seraphs attending; shouts, shouts filling the air;
Down, down swiftly from heaven Jesus our Lord will appear;
Yes, yes, oh yes! Jesus our Lord will appear.

Now, now, through a glass darkly, shine, shine visions to come;
Soon, soon we shall behold Him, cloudless and bright in our
   home;
Yes, yes, oh yes! cloudless and bright in our home.

Long, long, have we been waiting, who, who love His blest
   name;
Now, now, we are delighting, Jesus is near to proclaim;
Yes, yes, oh yes! Jesus is near to proclaim.

Anonymous

Still, still rest on the promise; cling, cling fast to His word;
Wait, wait, if He should tarry, we'll patiently wait for the
     Lord;
Yes, yes, oh yes! we'll patiently wait for the Lord.

Ned Wrights' Hymnbook, 1870

Anonymous

THE SAILOR'S HYMN

You sons of the main, that sail over the flood,
Whose sins, large as mountains, have reached up to God,
Remember the short voyage of life will soon end,
So now, brother sailors make Jesus your friend.

Look astern on your life—see your way marked with sin,
Look a-head, see what danger your soul it is in,
And the hard rocks of death beat fast on your knee,
Then your vessel and cargo will sink in the sea.

Lay by your old compass, it will do you no good,
It will never direct you the right way to God;
Mind your helm, brother sailor, and don't fall asleep,
Watch and pray, night and day, lest you sink in the deep.

Spring your luff, brother sailors, the breeze is now fair,
Trim your sails to the windward these torments you'll clear,
Your lading star, Jesus, keep full in your view,
And you'll weather all dangers—he will guide you safe through.

Denounce your old captain the devil, straight-way,
Or the crew that you sail with will lead you astray,
Desert the black colours, cross onto the red,
There Jesus is captain, to conquest He'll lead.

Your standards unfurl'd that waves through the air,
And volunteers are coming from far off and near,
Now's your time, brother sailors, no longer delay,
Embark now with Jesus, good wages He'll pay.

The bounty He will give you, when your voyage does begin,
He will forgive your transgressions and cleanse you from sin,
Good usage He will give you, while you sail on your way,
And shortly you will anchor in heaven's broad bay.

Your tarpaulin jackets no longer you will wear,
But robes dipped in heaven, all clean, white and fair,
And a new crown on your head that will appear like the sun,
And from glory to glory eternal will run.

In the harbour of glory for ever you will ride,
Free from all dangers and sins wrapp'd with tide,
Waves of death seem to roll, but the tempest is o'er,
And the hoarse breath of Boreas dismast thee no more.

A broadsheet, about 1870?

Elizabeth Cecilia Clephane. 1830–1869

There were ninety and nine that safely lay
    In the shelter of the fold;
And one was out on the hills, away
    Far off from the gates of gold—
    Away on the mountains wild and bare,
    Away from the tender Shepherd's care.

Lord, thou hast here thy ninety and nine,
    Are they not enough for thee?
But the Shepherd made answer, "This of mine
    Has wandered away from me.
    And although the road be rough and steep,
    I go to the desert to find my sheep."

But none of the ransomed ever knew
  How deep were the waters crossed,
Nor how dark the night that the Lord passed through,
  Ere he found his sheep that was lost
  Out in the desert he heard its cry,
  Sick and helpless and ready to die.

Lord, whence are those blood-drops all the way
  That mark out the mountain track?
They were shed for one that had gone astray
  Ere the Shepherd could bring him back.
  Lord, whence are thy hands so rent and torn?
  They are pierced to-night by many a thorn.

And all through the mountains, thunder-riven,
  And up from the rocky steep,
There rose a cry to the gates of heaven,
  "Rejoice, I have found my sheep!"
  And the Angels echoed around the throne,
  "Rejoice, for the Lord hath found his own."

Family Treasury, 1874

Philipp "P.P." Bliss. 1838–1876

His armour-bearer said . . . I am with thee according to thy heart.
1 Sam. xiv. 7

Only an armour-bearer, firmly I stand,
Waiting to follow at the King's command;
Marching, if "Onward" shall the order be,
Standing by my Captain, serving faithfully.

Hear ye the battle-cry! "Forward!" the call;
See, see the falt'ring ones, backward they fall.
Surely my Captain may depend on me,
Though but an armour-bearer I may be.

Only an armour-bearer, now in the field,
Guarding a shining helmet, sword, and shield,
Waiting to hear the thrilling battle-cry,
Ready then to answer, "Master, here am I."

Only an armour-bearer, yet may I share
Glory immortal, and a bright crown wear:
If in the battle to my trust I'm true,
Mine shall be the honours in the Grand Review.

Almost thou persuadest me to be a Christian. Acts xxvi. 28

"Almost persuaded" now to believe;
"Almost persuaded" Christ to receive;
Seems now some soul to say,
"Go, Spirit, go Thy way,
Some more convenient day
　　　On Thee I'll call."

"Almost persuaded," come, come today;
"Almost persuaded," turn not away;
Jesus invites you here,
Angels are ling'ring near,
Prayers rise from hearts so dear;
　　　O wand'rer, come!

"Almost persuaded," harvest is past!
"Almost persuaded," doom comes at last!
"Almost" cannot avail;
"Almost" is but to fail!
Sad, sad, that bitter wail—
　　　"Almost—*but lost!*"

Wherefore, my beloved, work out your own salvation with fear and trembling. Phil. ii. 12

Light in the darkness, sailor,
    Day is at hand!
See o'er the foaming billows
    Fair Haven's land;
Drear was the voyage, sailor,
    Now almost o'er;
Safe within the lifeboat, sailor,
    Pull for the shore.

    Pull for the shore, sailor,
        Pull for the shore!
    Heed not the rolling waves,
        But bend to the oar;
    Safe in the lifeboat, sailor,
        Cling to self no more!
    Leave the poor old stranded wreck,
        And pull for the shore.

Trust in the lifeboat, sailor;
    All else will fail:
Stronger the surges dash
    And fiercer the gale.
Heed not the stormy winds,
    Though loudly they roar;
Watch the "Bright and Morning Star,"
    And pull for the shore.

Bright gleams the morning, sailor,
    Uplift the eye;
Clouds and darkness disappearing,
    Glory is nigh!
Safe in the lifeboat, sailor,
    Sing evermore:
"Glory, glory, hallelujah!"
    Pull for the shore.

That which ye have hold fast till I come. Rev. ii. 25

Ho, my comrades! see the signal
 Waving in the sky!
Reinforcements now appearing,
 Victory is nigh!

 "Hold the fort, for I am coming!"
  Jesus signals still;
 Wave the answer back to heaven,
  "By Thy grace we will!"

See the mighty host advancing,
 Satan leading on;
Mighty men around us falling,
 Courage almost gone!

See the glorious banner waving!
 Hear the trumpet blow!
In our Leader's name we'll triumph
 Over every foe!

Fierce and long the battle rages,
 But our help is near;
Onward comes our great Commander,
 Cheer, my comrades, cheer!

James M. Black

WHEN THE ROLL IS CALLED UP YONDER

For the trumpet shall sound. 1 Cor. xv. 52

When the trumpet of the Lord shall sound, and time shall be
  no more,
And the morning breaks, eternal, bright and fair;
When the saved of earth shall gather over on the other shore,
And the roll is call'd up yonder, I'll be there.

When the roll is called up yonder,
When the roll is called up yonder,
When the roll is called up yonder,
When the roll is called up yonder,
   I'll be there.

On that bright and cloudless morning, when the dead in Christ
   shall rise,
And the glory of His resurrection share;
When His chosen ones shall gather to their home beyond the
   skies,
And the roll is call'd up yonder, I'll be there.

Let me labour for the Master from the dawn till setting sun,
Let me talk of all His wondrous love and care;
Then, when all of life is over, and my work on earth is done,
And the roll is call'd up yonder, I'll be there.

Robert Lowry. 1826–1899

SHALL WE GATHER AT THE RIVER?

A pure river of water of life, clear as crystal. Revelation xxii. 1

Shall we gather at the river,
   Where bright angel-feet have trod,
With its crystal tide for ever
   Flowing by the throne of God?

   Yes, we'll gather at the river,
   The beautiful, the beautiful river;
   Gather with the saints at the river,
   That flows by the throne of God.

On the margin of the river,
   Washing up its silver spray,
We will walk and worship ever,
   All the happy, golden day.

Ere we reach the shining river,
    Lay we ev'ry burden down;
Grace our spirits will deliver,
    And provide a robe and crown.

At the shining of the river,
    Mirror of the Saviour's face,
Saints, whom death will never sever,
    Raise their songs of saving grace.

Soon we'll reach the silver river,
    Soon our pilgrimage will cease;
Soon our happy hearts will quiver
    With the melody of peace.

Edgar Page Stites. b. 1837

BEULAH LAND

A land of corn and wine. Deut. xxxiii. 28

I've reached the land of corn and wine,
And all its riches freely mine;
Here shines undimm'd one blissful day,
For all my night has passed away.

    O Beulah Land, sweet Beulah Land,
    As on thy highest mount I stand,
    I look away across the sea,
    Where mansions are prepared for me,
    And view the shining glory shore:
    My heaven, my home for evermore!

My Saviour comes and walks with me,
And sweet communion here have we;
He gently leads me by His hand,
For this is heaven's borderland.

A sweet perfume upon the breeze
Is borne from ever-vernal trees;
And flowers that, never fading, grow
Where streams of life for ever flow.

The zephyrs seem to float to me
Sweet sounds of heaven's melody,
As angels with the white-robed throng
Join in the sweet redemption song.

1876

Elisha A. Hoffman. b. 1839

HAVE YOU BEEN TO JESUS?

Wash me, and I shall be whiter than snow. Psalm li. 7

Have you been to Jesus for the cleansing power?
    Are you wash'd in the blood of the Lamb?
Are you fully trusting in His grace this hour?
    Are you wash'd in the blood of the Lamb?

    Are you wash'd in the blood—
    In the soul-cleansing blood of the Lamb?
    Are your garments spotless?
    Are they white as snow?
    Are you wash'd in the blood of the Lamb?

Are you walking daily by the Saviour's side?
    Are you wash'd in the blood of the Lamb?
Do you rest each moment in the Crucified?
    Are you wash'd in the blood of the Lamb?

When the Bridgegroom cometh will your robes be white?
    Pure and white in the blood of the Lamb?
Will your soul be ready for the mansions bright
    And be washed in the blood of the Lamb?

Lay aside the garments that are stained with sin,
    And be washed in the blood of the Lamb!
There's a fountain flowing for the soul unclean—
    Oh, be washed in the blood of the Lamb.

Frances Jane Crosby. 1820–1915

COME, OH COME, WITH THY BROKEN HEART!

If any man thirst, let him come unto Me. John vii. 37

> Come, oh come, with thy broken heart,
> Weary and worn with care;
> Come and kneel at the open door,
> Jesus is waiting there:
> Waiting to heal thy wounded soul.
> Waiting to give thee rest:
> Why wilt thou walk where shadows fall?
> Come to His loving breast!
>
> Firmly cling to the blessed cross,
> There shall thy refuge be;
> Wash thee now in the crimson fount,
> Flowing so pure for thee:
> List to the gentle warning voice!
> List to the earnest call!
> Leave at the cross thy burden now:
> Jesus will bear it all.
>
> Come and taste of the precious feast,
> Feast of eternal love;
> Think of joys that for ever bloom,
> Bright in the life above:
> Come with a trusting heart to God,
> Come and be saved by grace;
> Come, for He longs to clasp thee now
> Close in His dear embrace.

WELCOME FOR ME!

When he was a great way off his father saw him. Luke xv. 20

Like a bird on the deep, far away from its nest,
    I had wander'd, my Saviour, from Thee;
But Thy kind, loving voice call'd me home to Thy breast,
    And I knew there was welcome for me!

    Welcome for me, Saviour, from Thee!
    A welcome, glad welcome for me!
    Now, like a dove, I rest in Thy love,
    And find a sweet refuge in Thee.

I am safe in the Ark; I have folded my wings
    On the bosom of mercy Divine;
I am fill'd with delight by Thy presence so bright,
    And the joy that will ever be mine.

Now in Jesus I rest, and I dread not the storm,
    Tho' around me the surges may roll;
I will look to the skies, where the day never dies,
    I will sing of the joy in my soul.

RESCUE THE PERISHING

Go out into the highways and hedges, and compel them to come in, that My house may be filled. Luke xiv. 23

    Rescue the perishing,
    Care for the dying
Snatch them in pity from sin and the grave;
    Weep o'er the erring one,
    Lift up the fallen,
Tell them of Jesus, the Mighty to save.

Rescue the perishing,
Care for the dying;
Jesus is merciful,
Jesus will save.

Tho' they are slighting Him,
 Still He is waiting,
Waiting the penitent child to receive,
 Plead with them earnestly,
 Plead with them gently;
He will forgive if they only believe.

 Down in the human heart,
 Crushed by the tempter,
Feelings lie buried that grace can restore;
 Touched by a loving hand,
 Wakened by kindness,
Chords that were broken will vibrate once more.

 Rescue the perishing,
 Duty demands it;
Strength for thy labour the Lord will provide:
 Back to the narrow way
 Patiently win them;
Tell the poor wanderer a Saviour has died.

BLESSED ASSURANCE

Beloved, now are we the sons of God. 1 John iii. 2

Blessed assurance—Jesus is mine!
 Oh, what a foretaste of glory Divine!
Heir of salvation, purchase of God;
 Born of His Spirit, washed in His blood.

> *This is my story, this is my song,*
> *Praising my Saviour all the day long;*
> *This is my story, this is my song,*
> *Praising my Saviour all the day long.*

Perfect submission, perfect delight,
    Visions of rapture burst on my sight;
Angels descending, bring from above,
    Echoes of mercy, whispers of love.

Perfect submission, all is at rest,
    I in my Saviour am happy and blest;
Watching and waiting, looking above,
    Filled with His goodness, lost in His love.

SAVED BY GRACE

By grace ye are saved. Ephesians ii. 5

Some day the silver cord will break,
    And I no more as now shall sing;
But oh, the joy when I shall wake
    Within the palace of the King!

> *And I shall see Him face to face,*
> *And tell the story—Saved by grace;*
> *And I shall see Him face to face,*
> *And tell the story—Saved by grace.*

Some day my earthly house will fall,
    I cannot tell how soon 't will be;
But this I know—my All in All
    Has now a place in heaven for me.

Some day, when fades the golden sun
    Beneath the rosy-tinted west,
My blessed Lord shall say, "Well done!"
    And I shall enter into rest.

Some day; till then I'll watch and wait—
    My lamp all trimmed and burning bright—
That when my Saviour opes the gate,
    My soul to Him may take its flight.

Ira D. Sankey's Sacred Songs and Solos, 1912

George Bennard

On a hill far away stood an old rugged Cross,
    The emblem of suffering and shame,
And I love that old Cross where the dearest and best
    For a world of lost sinners was slain.

    So I'll cherish the old rugged Cross
        Till my trophies at last I lay down:
    I will cling to the old rugged Cross
        And exchange it some day for a crown.

O that old rugged Cross, so despised by the world,
    Has a wondrous attraction for me;
For the dear Lamb of God left His glory above
    To bear it to dark Calvary.

To the old rugged Cross I will ever be true,
    Its shame and reproach gladly bear;
Then He'll call me some day to my home far away
    Where His glory for ever I'll share.

The Song Book of the Salvation Army, 1953

Index of Authors

Index of First Lines

A

309

Index

Index

H

I

Index

J

K

L

M

N

T